Cooking With Courgettes

Delicious Recipes, Preserves and
More With Courgettes

Jason Johns

Visit me at www.GardeningWithJason.com for gardening tips and advice or follow me at www.YouTube.com/OwningAnAllotment for my video diary and tips. Join me on Facebook at www.Facebook.com/OwningAnAllotment.

Follow me on Instagram and Twitter as @allotmentowner for regular updates, tips and to ask your gardening questions.

If you have enjoyed this book, please leave a review on Amazon. I read each review personally and the feedback helps me to continually improve my books and provide you with more helpful books to read.

Once you have read this book, you will be offered a chance to download one of my books for free. Please turn to the back of the book to find out how to get your free book.

TABLE OF CONTENTS

INTRODUCTION

One of the most popular vegetables to grow at home is the zucchini or courgette plant. The fruits are relatively expensive to buy in the stores, particularly out of season, yet the seeds are cheap and the plant extremely easy to grow. A single plant can produce twenty or thirty fruits in a season, and most people grow several plants.

You can easily end up with too many courgettes and no idea what to do with them. In the past, I have literally given them away in the streets when walking home from my allotment as I have had so many.

Zucchini and courgette are exactly the same things. Americans tend to use the word zucchini to describe a courgette while Europeans would just say courgette. In reality, zucchini is a variety of courgette, popular in the United States and most often found in stores there. There are many more varieties of courgette on the market other than just zucchini, and many of them are really very tasty! In this book, we will use the word courgette when referring to this plant and it's fruit for clarity and ease of reading.

This book is not only about what to do with the traditional green courgette, but also to encourage you to grow your own courgettes and try the many different varieties that are out there. My personal favourites are the traditionally shaped courgettes but yellow in colour and any of the round varieties. However, as you learn about the different varieties, you will decide which ones you want to try for yourself, depending on your location and your growing conditions.

Not only will this book to encourage you to experiment growing courgettes, but it is going to give you a lot of ideas on what to do with this remarkably versatile vegetable. Most people will throw it in a stir-fry or ratatouille, not realizing just how much you can do with this vegetable. The flowers, for example, are often ignored by growers, yet are a delicacy that will cost you a lot of money if you ever see them on the menu in a restaurant. Yet most of us ignore them or throw them away!

However, courgettes are very versatile, and one of the best dishes you can make with them is a chocolate cake! Trust me … it is fantastic, and people will not believe you've put courgette in it!

There are lots of uses for courgettes, which you will learn all about in this book. I encourage you to try the many different recipes and experiment. There are lots you can do and after the first few courgettes, trust me, you will be pleased for these recipes and to have some variety!

Growing courgettes is surprisingly easy, and anyone can do it. They are not particularly demanding vegetables, nor do they require masses of space. In fact, the bush varieties will comfortably grow in a large pot on a balcony or patio, so anyone can grow them, whether you live in a city or the suburbs.

Have fun with these recipes and let me know how you get on with them! I'd love to hear which are your favourites. There are plenty of recipes to choose from, and the book is broken down into sections depending on the type of meal you want to cook. Feel free to adjust the recipes to your personal tastes, including using reduced fat ingredients if you want to keep the calorie count down.

Happy courgette cooking, and when you have finished the book, please remember to leave a review to let me know what you thought about it.

GROWING YOUR OWN COURGETTES

Growing your own courgettes is surprisingly easy to do. All you need is a packet of seeds of your chosen variety, some small pots (to start with) and some compost. In your local stores you will find two or three varieties of courgette at most, usually a green one, a yellow one and perhaps one other.

If you want to buy the more unusual varieties, then you will have to go online to the specialist seed providers where you will find as many as a couple of dozen varieties. I can recommend the more unusual, heritage varieties, rather than the F1 breeds as the heritage varieties usually have a much better taste.

When your courgettes mature, it is best to pick them when they are around the size you would see in the stores or a little larger. If you leave them too long, then they grow far too big. The skin then becomes tough, and the centre becomes inedible as the seeds form. However, if you do let your courgettes grow large, and believe me, they will, then you can still use them in cooking. Just peel the skin off and scoop out the stringy middle bit where the seeds are. Yellow varieties do not tend to grow as large as the green varieties and will usually just become tougher, containing more seeds. Be aware that some of the green varieties can double in size over night.

Regularly picking the courgettes will encourage your plants to continue to produce more fruit and you will have a long and bountiful growing season. One plant will easily produce courgettes for a couple of months if you regularly harvest them.

If you want your courgette plants to do really well, and this applies to any member of the squash family, you need to prepare the planting site. This is done by digging holes three feet (around 90cm) apart that are about a spade deep and wide. Dig one per courgette plant. These are filled with well-rotted manure and compost, then sprinkled with chicken manure pellets or a general purpose fertilizer.

The courgettes are planted either direct or as seedlings above these pits. If you are well organized, then you can prepare the site as summer ends, filling the pit with manure and compostable materials which will break down over winter ready for spring planting.

You can grow in containers or grow bags, just be aware that courgettes are greedy and thirsty plants that will need a lot of watering and feeding, more so when not in the ground. You will usually have a single plant per container and two per grow bag.

Start the seeds off indoors or under glass in small pots, one seed per pot. Keep the compost moist, but not wet. As the seed grows, you will need to move it to a larger pot so that it doesn't get pot bound.

Courgette plants should not be planted out until the risk of frost has passed as they are extremely susceptible to frost damage. The last frost date in your area can be found out by searching online. If you have any worries about a late frost, then cover your plants with some horticultural fleece. This should protect them from the frost and prevent any damage.

The courgettes are planted in the holes you prepared earlier, one per hole. Plant them firmly and securely, then water them in, careful not to get water on the leaves. For the first couple of weeks after planting, water the plants regularly and make sure they are kept moist but not soaking wet. Once they have established a strong root system, you can water them less frequently.

My best advice with courgettes is to plant two seeds every 7 to 14 days. This means that your plants will mature at different times, so you get a longer spread of fruit throughout the growing season. With this method, you can enjoy fresh courgettes all summer and up until the first frost.

Before planting your courgettes out, you need to harden them off for a week or two. This basically means you leave them outside during the day, moving them back indoors at night. Over time, you leave them out more and more, until they are out all night (avoiding the risk of frost) and then you plant them out in the ground. This acclimatizes them to being outdoors. Planting your courgettes straight out will shock them which can stunt their growth or even kill them.

Once the plants are established, you need to regularly feed and water them. Do not get water on the leaves otherwise, you will encourage the development of powdery mildew, which can kill your plants. Water directly to the roots of the plants. I will usually drive a pipe or upturned soda bottle into the ground by the roots and water through that, which means the courgette plant does not sit in any water which can rot the neck of the plant.

When the fruits start to form, feed your plants around every 10 days with a high potash liquid fertilizer which will encourage the development of healthy fruits.

If you are growing indoors or under glass, then you might have to pollinate your plants by hand as insects may not be able to get to the flowers. This means carefully taking pollen from a male plant and rubbing it on the stamen of a female plant, using a cotton bud or small paint brush. Alternatively, leave the greenhouse door or windows open to encourage pollinators to come in and do the business for you.

Pick your courgettes when they are the size of those you see in the stores. Try not to leave them on the plant too long because they will become too big, which can spoil the flavour. Regular harvesting will ensure the plant keeps producing new fruits for longer, giving you a larger crop.

Common Growing Problems

Courgettes, like many plants, suffer from their fair share of diseases. Most are pretty easy to avoid by looking after them properly. It is worth keeping your eyes out for these problems because if you take action as you spot the issue, you are more likely to save your plant.

These are the most commonly found problems, but there are many others out there. Most, you will never see, but if your plants show any other symptoms of disease you can search online and determine what is wrong. The below problems are the ones that are most likely to affect you as a home gardener.

Slugs & Snails
These are probably going to be your number one enemy while growing courgettes. Although the do not damage the leaves, they will happily chew through the fruit, particularly where it is touching the ground. For the less squeamish of you, you can cut around those parts, but many people would rather not eat them.

Unfortunately, there isn't a huge amount you can do against slugs and snails. Slug pellets are very effective, but some people prefer not to use these because they can harm other wildlife or pets plus they are not organic.

Beer traps are quite effective, but they need emptying regularly, and they stink to high heaven on hot days. You need a few to ensure you get the slugs, but they do work, though I have seen drunk slugs trying getting out of beer traps. You sink a container into the ground, with the lip slightly above ground level and fill it three-quarters full with cheap beer (don't waste the good stuff!). Change them every few days.

Going out at dawn or dusk with a torch and picking the slugs and snails off your plants is the most effective way of controlling them, but not everyone is willing to do this. Do this every day for a few days, and you will quickly reduce your pest population. Just remember to dispose of them far away from your garden so they cannot make their way back to your courgette plants.

Copper tape, egg shells, coffee grounds and many of these other techniques aren't particularly effective in controlling slugs or snails. Having tried them all, they are more work than they are worth and I've seen snails happily sliding over crushed egg shells to get to my seedlings!

Encouraging hedgehogs, frogs, and toads into your garden is one way of controlling slugs, but you need to avoid using slug pellets as they are poisonous to these beneficial animals. Although these will eat some of the pests, they are unlikely to eat them all, so using other control methods is recommended.

Chickens also like to eat slugs. The downside of these is that slugs like to eat your seedlings ... and so do chickens. Many a home gardener has allowed their chickens loose in their vegetable plot to control slugs only to find their seedlings have also been eaten by the hungry birds.

Powdery Mildew
This is a big problem for all members of the squash family and appears as a powdery, white deposit on the surface of the leaves. Over time, the leaves shrivel, and their growth is affected. It can spread to stalks and will kill your plants.

Powdery mildew is a fungal infection that is caused by the plant's leaves being damp on warm, humid summer nights. It is often caused by the exuberant gardener watering his or her courgette plants in the evening and splashing water all over the leaves. The leaves do not have time to dry out before night falls, and this encourages the development of the fungus that causes powdery mildew.

Water your plants in the morning, direct to the roots if you can. If you have to water in the evening, which many of us do due to work commitments, then water direct to the base of the plant, avoiding splashing any water on the leaves. It will help if you put a pipe or soda bottle at the base of the plant as then you can water the roots directly with no chance of getting the leaves wet.

There are chemical sprays and home remedies you can use on powdery mildew, but in my experience, they are of limited effectiveness. Rather than cure the problem, they just seem to stop it from getting worse. Prevention is far better than a cure here, and good water management will help reduce the risk of this disease.

No Fruit or Fruit Rotting
If your plant doesn't produce any fruit or the fruit rots when it is very small, then this isn't a pest or disease but caused by the weather. It usually happens when the first months of summer are too cool and damp, so the plant doesn't get pollinated correctly.

In most cases, this will solve itself when the weather improves, but you can help the problem along by hand pollinating the flowers. Pick off a male flower (there is no swelling at the base of a male flower) and brush the central part of it against the middle of the female flowers, which do have swellings at the base (which will become courgettes). You can also grow flowers around your courgette plants to attract pollinating insects. This problem is more common with courgette grown in a greenhouse or hoop house as pollinators cannot get to the plants.

Grey Mould

This is usually a problem when the weather is wet and damp and usually affects damaged or unhealthy plants. However, it can affect any plant given the right conditions. You will see a fuzzy grey mould growing on buds, leaves, fruits, and flowers, which will cause the infected plants to die eventually. More often than not this disease enters the plant through a wound, so be careful you do not break any leaves or stalks while tending them.

By ensuring your plants are spaced correctly you will allow the air to circulate, which helps to prevent this disease. Remember, courgette plants can grow quite big, so your frugal spacing may cause you problems later down the line. Check the seed packets to determine how far apart to space your plants.

Lack of Female Flowers

The female flowers are the ones that produce the courgette fruit and can be identified by a swelling, which is the immature fruit, at the base of the flower. When the temperature is too low early in the growing season, your plant will mainly produce male flowers. If the season remains cold, then it will produce few female flowers. Usually though, as the weather warms up, the production of male and female flowers evens out.

Avoid planting your courgette plants out too early as the cooler temperatures can encourage the production of male flowers. Fleece your plants on cooler nights to help protect them from the cold. Ensure the plants are located somewhere that gets a lot of sunlight during the day to help keep them warm.

Unfortunately, if the growing season is too cold then you will get very few female flowers. You should consider either moving your plants into a greenhouse or fleecing them to see if that warms them up enough to produce female flowers. In either of these situations, be prepared to hand pollinate your plants.

Lack of Male Flowers

This can happen if the temperatures are too high and can be avoided by not planting out too late. Avoid planting out after mid-summer, and you will reduce the risk of producing only female flowers. Make sure there is sufficient ventilation if you are growing under glass as this will help keep the temperature down.

Bitter Fruit

Occasionally, you will find a plant produces fruit that is bitter. This is because it has produced too much of the chemicals used to protect itself. Most commonly this is due to a mutation in the plant and happens in saved seeds. I'd recommend removing and destroying any plants that have this issue. If you are saving your seeds, it may only be one or two plants that are affected.

Fungal Diseases

There are a variety of potential fungal diseases other than those we discussed above. You can reduce the risk of fungal diseases by:

- Regularly watering your plant direct to the roots, avoiding getting water on the leaves
- Mulch around the base of your plants to prevent moisture loss through evaporation, leaving an area around the stem that is mulch free to prevent the stalk from rotting
- Space your plants correctly so air can flow properly around them

One common fungal disease is Verticillium Wilt, which causes the upper parts of the plants to wilt and die. Unfortunately, there is no known cure for this, and the plant should be removed and destroyed, along with the soil from the area around the roots.

Good water management practice will generally prevent fungal infections from taking hold.

Viral Problems

There are a number of viral diseases that can affect courgette plants including the mosaic virus (causes yellow mottling on the leaves). There is very little you can do if a plant does become infected apart from remove and destroy it. Buying your seeds from a reputable supplier will ensure they are disease free.

Take care to avoid damaging your plant as any open wounds can allow viral infections to take hold. Aphid infestations also often introduce viruses into your plants, so regularly check for aphids and treat the plant the moment you see any.

Pests

There are a few pests that bother courgette plants. We've talked about aphids, slugs, and snails which are by far the worst. Deer and rabbit can be partial to a courgette, so you need to take precautions if they are in your area. Red spider mite and glasshouse whitefly are two other common pests. However, these rarely have a chance to build up to a size where they will cause serious damage to your plant. Check regularly for either of these pests and treat if you need to.

THE DIFFERENT VARIETIES OF COURGETTE

There are a lot of different types of courgette available and which you grow will depend on your personal preference. In the stores, you are likely going to find the same two or three varieties which are popular, easy to grow and transport well. If you buy online from seed shops, you will find more varieties, including some of the unusual and more interesting types.

Here are some of the more common varieties, though there are plenty of others available. Some of these are what is known as open pollinated, and others are F1 hybrid plants. You cannot save seeds from an F1 hybrid plant because they will not always grow true to the original plant, meaning you cannot guarantee you get the same variety the following year. F1 hybrid varieties are bred from two plants for specific traits and will grow well for you, producing a good crop. Some F1 varieties have resistance to diseases or pests, so they are useful if your area suffers from those. Often F1 seeds are infertile and will not grow.

Open pollinated varieties, which are normally heirloom varieties, have been bred over a number of generations of the plant. This means that when you save the seeds from your courgette, they are fertile and will grow the following year producing the plant you gathered the seeds from. If you are planning on saving any seeds, then you should only buy open pollinated varieties. Check the seed packet if you are unsure as it will tell you which type of courgette it is.

Which seeds you choose will depend on the type of courgette you want to grow and the space available. Some varieties are bush varieties, meaning they are compact and ideal for small spaces or containers. Other varieties trail and will grow much larger, needing a larger growing area.

Depending on where you live, you may want to choose a variety that has some disease resistance. The seed packets will tell you what resistance they have, and many disease resistant varieties will be F1 hybrid seeds. However, if your area suffers from the mosaic virus or powdery mildew, then a disease resistant variety can mean the difference between harvesting from your plants or having to destroy them.

- Black Beauty – a popular open pollinated variety that takes about 110 days to mature. It produces lovely, glossy green fruits with a long harvest period. This is a compact bush variety, ideal for containers. The fruit is best harvested at around 8" long.
- Raven – an F1 hybrid that only takes about 48 days to mature. It produces dark green fruits that are high in the antioxidant, lutein which protects the eyes from UV light. The bushes are compact, and you will get as many as three fruits per week, so you don't get overwhelmed by courgettes. The fruits are best harvested at between 6 and 8 inches long, though the skins remain tender up to about 10" long.
- Fordhook – an open pollinated variety that matures in around 57 days. A bushy plant will spread as much as five feet. The courgettes from this plant are excellent and best harvested when no longer than 8" long.
- Dunja – an F1 hybrid variety, taking around 47 days to mature. It produces a very good yield of dark green fruit. This variety has a degree of resistance to powdery mildew, courgette yellow mosaic virus, papaya ringspot virus and watermelons mosaic virus.
- Gadzukes – another F1 hybrid variety that matures in around 55 days. It is an Italian-style courgette and has light green ridges, growing on an upright, compact bush.
- Gourmet Gold – an F1 hybrid variety, maturing in 55 days and producing orange to yellow coloured fruits. This variety has a long harvesting season and has some resistance to viral infections.
- Cocozelle – an open pollinated, heirloom variety that matures in

just 50 days. The vines are quite compact, so they are ideal for smaller places. The fruit is fantastic, being still tender up to about a foot long.

- Caserta – an open pollinated, heirloom variety which matures in 65 days with lighter coloured courgette. This is a very high yielding plant yet grows on a compact bush. You can harvest fruit from this plant up to 16" long, and they are still tender and delicious.

- Magda – an F1 hybrid, maturing in a short time of just 48 days. It has a dense, nutty flavoured fruit that is great cooked or grilled. The plants are tall and bushy, with the fruit best harvested when smaller, no more than 4" in size.

- Summer Green Tiger – an F1 hybrid that matures in 60 days producing lovely green fruit with a dark green stripe. A very popular and tasty courgette that can be harvested up to 8" in length. This variety is a compact, bushy vine and so is ideal for containers or small spaces.

- Italian Ribbed – an open pollinated, heirloom variety that matures in 58 days to produce a very popular, ridged courgette that is ideal roasted or cooked. The vines are large, spreading to as much as 5' in size and the fruit are best harvested no longer than 8".

- Bush Baby – an F1 hybrid that matures in 55 days, producing fruit best harvested no longer than 6" in length. The fruits are a deep green colour with lighter green stripes. This compact bush plant is ideal for containers and produces a courgette that is superb when grilled.

- Patio Star – another F1 hybrid, maturing in 50 days. This compact bush starts fruiting early and has a long season.

- Golden Egg – an F1 hybrid that matures in 45 days, producing lovely yellow egg shaped courgettes. It has an incredible taste and is very popular in cooking because of it. The vines are large, spreading as much as 6', producing fruit for around eight weeks. The courgette from this plant are best harvested at about 4" in length.

- Round De Nice – an heirloom variety that is open pollinated, maturing in 45 days. The fruits from this compact vine are round and dark green, best harvested at between 3" and 4" in diameter. They are excellent stuffed.

COURGETTE FLOWER RECIPES

The flowers of the courgette plant are considered a delicacy and are absolutely delicious when cooked and eaten. Obviously, if you remove too many flowers then you will not get the fruits from the plant, but you can certainly remove and eat most of the male flowers and hand pollinate the female flowers.

Courgette flowers are rarely if ever, seen in a store to buy and will occasionally be served in high-class restaurants where they are an expensive dish to buy. The flowers do not store well, so all of these dishes are best made as soon as you pick the flowers.

Stuffed Courgette Flowers

This is one of the most common dishes made with courgette flowers and tastes fantastic. Feel free to half the recipe if you want to.

Ingredients:

- 8 courgette flowers with a small courgette fruit attached
- 9oz / 250g ricotta cheese
- 5¼oz / 150g soft goat's cheese
- 3½oz / 100g plain flour
- 1 cup / 200ml iced water
- 2 large tomatoes (deseeded and finely diced)
- 1 large egg
- ½ red chilli (de-seeded and finely chopped)
- 2 tablespoons extra virgin olive oil
- Pinch of bicarbonate of soda
- Zest of 1 lemon
- Handful of mint leaves (chopped)

Method:

1. Make the batter by whisking the flour, bicarbonate of soda and egg together in a wide bowl
2. Whisking continuously, gradually add the ice water until the batter is smooth and has a consistency similar to that of double cream
3. In another bowl, mix both the cheeses, the chilli, lemon zest and some of the chopped mint leaves, seasoning to taste; this is the filling
4. In a third bowl, mix the tomatoes, olive oil and rest of the mint leaves, seasoning to taste; this is the dressing
5. Carefully open up each flower and remove the stamen, if it is there
6. Fill the flower with the filling
7. Close the flower and twist the petal ends to seal it
8. Heat oil for deep frying, either a deep fat fryer or oil in a large saucepan
9. In batches, cover the flowers in batter then fry for about 2 minutes
10. Flip, using a slotted spoon, frying for a further two minutes until they are crisp
11. Place on kitchen paper to drain, leave somewhere warm until all the flowers are fried
12. Serve sprinkled with salt and with the dressing arranged in a circle

around the flowers

Deep-Fried Courgette Flowers

This is another variation on the stuffed and deep fried courgette flowers.

Ingredients:
- 8 to 12 courgette flowers
- 3½oz / 100g ricotta cheese
- 3½oz / 100g plain flour
- 1½oz /40g cornflour
- 1 cup / 200ml ice cold water
- 2 tablespoons Parmesan cheese (grated)
- Handful fresh mixed herbs (finely chopped)
- ½ teaspoon baking powder
- ½ teaspoon salt
- Nasturtiums or other edible flowers (optional garnish)

Method:
1. Make the filling by beating the ricotta cheese until it becomes soft and smooth
2. Stir in the Parmesan and mixed herbs, seasoning to taste with salt and pepper
3. Put 2 to 4 teaspoons of filling in each flower, twisting the petals carefully to hold the mixture in place
4. Sift the flour, baking powder, salt and cornflour into a bowl
5. Gradually add the water, whisking continuously as you do, aiming for a consistency similar to single cream; do not over-mix
6. Heat your oil in a deep fat fryer or large saucepan
7. Dip the stuffed flowers into the batter and cook for a couple of minutes until crispy and golden brown
8. Drain on kitchen paper while cooking the rest of the flowers
9. Serve sprinkled with sea salt and decorated with edible flowers

Penne Paste with Courgette Flowers

A fantastic, colourful dish that doesn't involve deep frying the courgette flowers.

Ingredients:

- 16 courgette flowers (torn in half)
- 9oz / 225g penne pasta (or substitute for any type of pasta)
- 8fl oz / 240ml vegetable stock
- 1oz / 30g Parmesan cheese (grated)
- 8 tablespoons olive oil
- 20 fresh basil leaves
- 2 anchovy fillets
- 2 small courgette (finely sliced lengthwise)
- 2 small onions (finely sliced)
- 2 garlic cloves (whole but bashed)
- Salt and freshly ground black pepper
- Extra virgin olive oil (for drizzling)

Method:

1. Fry the garlic in the oil until golden in colour
2. Remove the garlic and put to one side
3. Fry the anchovy fillets and break them up with a wooden spoon
4. Add the onions, and sweat for a couple of minutes
5. Add the courgette and four labels of vegetable stock
6. Stir well, then add the basil leaves and courgette flowers
7. Fry, stirring often, for a couple of minutes
8. Taste and season appropriately
9. Cook the pasta until it is al-dente, then drain
10. Mix the pasta into the sauce and stir in the Parmesan cheese
11. Serve drizzled with olive oil

Spicy Crab Courgette Flowers

This is an unusual variation on stuffing courgette flowers. It's well worth a try if you like fresh crab.

Ingredients:
- 10 baby courgettes with the flowers still attached
- 1 red chilli (de-seeded and finely chopped)
- 3½oz / 100g white crab meat (fresh)
- 1 tablespoon extra-virgin olive oil
- 1 teaspoon flat leaf parsley (freshly chopped)
- 1 teaspoon white wine vinegar
- Salt and freshly ground black pepper to taste

Method:
1. Mix the crab meat with the chilli, parsley and white wine vinegar, seasoning to taste
2. Carefully fill the courgette flowers with between 2 and 4 teaspoons of the mixture
3. Twist the top of each flower to seal the mixture in
4. Heat the oil in your frying pan
5. In batches, cook the courgette, turning, for around 7 minutes – the flowers become dark orange in colour when cooked, careful not to overcook
6. Serve immediately

Hot Courgette Flowers

A lovely dish that combines the delicate flavour of the courgette flowers with the kick of horseradish. Montasio is a Venetian cheese that has a delicious, creamy flavour. It is made with animal rennet so vegetarians should seek any alternative mild and creamy cheese.

Ingredients:
- 36 courgette flowers
- 1 red bell pepper (de-seeded and cut into thin strips)
- 1 Granny Smith apple (grated)
- 4¼oz Montasio cheese (grated)
- 1¾oz butter
- 1 fresh horseradish root

Method:
1. Rinse the flowers, and place them upside down on kitchen paper to drain
2. Put half the butter into a pan and melt
3. Sauté the peppers until crisp
4. In a second pan, sauté the courgette flowers in the rest of the butter, until they just wilt slightly, then season with salt
5. Arrange the grated apple in a mound in the middle of a serving plate
6. Cover this with the cheese
7. Arrange the pepper strips on top of the cheese, followed by the courgette flowers
8. Grate some fresh horseradish over the top (wear gloves and be careful as horseradish is extremely hot)

Crispy Stuffed Courgette Flowers
This is a lovely way to stuff the flowers and is served with a basil sauce. The stuffing is a lovely tomato based sauce, and the flowers are coated with breadcrumbs. This is a bit more work than other dishes, but the resulting dish speaks for itself.

Stuffed Flower Ingredients:
- 4 courgette flowers
- 1 egg (beaten)
- 2 2/3oz Pandora breadcrumbs
- 1¾oz semi-firm cheese (cut into 4 rectangles)
- 2½fl oz vegetable oil

Tomato Stuffing Ingredients:
- 2 beefsteak tomatoes (peeled and chopped)
- 2 shallots (peeled and finely chopped)
- 1 carrot
- 1 garlic clove (minced)
- 1 bunch of basil
- 1 2/3fl oz extra virgin olive oil
- Salt and freshly ground black pepper

Basil Sauce Ingredients:
- 1oz / 25g Parmesan cheese (freshly grated)
- 1 garlic clove (peeled and chopped)
- 4 tablespoons pine nuts (toasted)
- Extra virgin olive oil (to taste)
- Handful fresh basil leaves

Garnish:
- Rocket
- Parmesan cheese shavings
- Toasted pine nuts

Method:
1. The stuffing recipe is made by heating the shallots and garlic in olive oil
2. Once softened, add the tomatoes and mix well
3. Tie the basil into a bunch and add this to the stuffing mixture
4. Cook for 3 to 5 minutes until the tomatoes begin to soften

5. Add the carrot (whole) which will help sweeten the dish
6. Cover the pan and cook until the mixture is soft and the tomatoes have begun to break down, about 5 minutes
7. Remove the carrot and basil, discarding, and season to taste
8. Keep the stuffing mixture warm until serving
9. To make the sauce, put the pine nuts, garlic, Parmesan and basil into a blender and process
10. Slowly pour in the olive oil while blending until it becomes a smooth sauce
11. Transfer the sauce into a small pan and warm before serving
12. Carefully remove the stamen from each of the courgette flowers
13. Stuff each flower with a piece of cheese, folding the petals to keep it inside
14. Dip each flower in the egg, then dredge in breadcrumbs, ensuring each flower is fully coated
15. Heat the oil in a pan and fry each flower for a few minutes, turning regularly, until crisp and golden all over
16. Drain on kitchen paper
17. Put some sauce on each plate, then add some of the stuffing to the middle of the plate, topping with a courgette flower and garnishing

RAW COURGETTE RECIPES

Courgettes are great cooked, but they are also delicious raw and can be used in a wide variety of dishes. The following are recipes that use raw courgette, and many are suitable for, or at least can be adjusted to be suitable for, vegans and followers of the Paleo diet. A lot of these dishes work really well if you use a combination of green and yellow courgette to add colour to the dishes.

Not commonly eaten raw, courgette is surprisingly tasty. Remember too that it can be served as simple vegetable batons along with carrots, cucumber, celery, and bell peppers with your favourite dip.

Courgette Noodles with Pesto

Courgettes makes delicious noodles that are a great alternative to pasta in this unusual dish. This recipe makes enough for two servings, but feel free to increase the quantities to make more.

Ingredients:

- 4 courgettes (two green and two yellow ideally)
- 1 avocado (peeled)
- 1 garlic clove
- Juice from ½ lemon
- ¼ teaspoon sea salt
- Freshly ground black pepper

Ingredients:

1. Cut the ends off the courgettes and turn into noodles with a spiralizer or food grater (you can use an attachment on your food processor)
2. Put the rest of the ingredients into your food processor and blend to make the pesto
3. In a large bowl, mix the noodles with the pesto, serving topped with pine nuts

Pesto Pasta
This is another interesting dish, combining courgette noodles with kelp
noodles. It's pretty quick to make and is perfect for lunch time. Feel free
to swap out the kelp noodles with any other type you prefer.

Ingredients:
- 4 courgettes (spiralized)
- 1 garlic clove
- ½ bunch fresh basil
- Juice of 1 lemon
- ½ cup pine nuts
- ¼ to ½ cup extra virgin olive oil (to taste)
- ¼ cup cashew nuts
- 1 tablespoon nutritional yeast
- 1 tablespoon apple cider vinegar
- ½ teaspoon salt
- Sweetener or sugar to taste
- Fresh spinach and cherry tomatoes for garnish

Method:
1. Put the kelp noodles and courgette into a large bowl and mix,
   before putting to one side
2. Put the rest of the ingredients into your blender and process until
   smooth
3. Add to the noodles and stir thoroughly, serving garnished with
   spinach and tomatoes

Creamy Pesto

Another great courgette noodle dish with a creamy pesto sauce. This recipe is quick to prepare and makes for a very filling lunch.

Ingredients:
- 2 courgettes (spiralized)
- 2 garlic cloves
- 2 cups fresh spinach
- 2 cups fresh basil
- ½ cup walnuts
- ¼ cup pine nuts
- 3 tablespoons extra virgin olive oil
- 2½ tablespoons nutritional yeast
- 1 teaspoon salt
- Lemon juice (optional – to taste)

Method:
1. Add all the ingredients, except the courgette, into your blender and process until smooth
2. Taste and adjust salt, pepper and lemon juice until the desired taste is achieved
3. Mix the pesto with the courgette and serve

Summer Salad Bowl
This is a wonderful salad, full of summer taste and makes a great lunch or side salad to a main meal.

Ingredients:
- 1 courgette
- 1 tomato
- 1 ear of corn
- 1 garlic clove (minced)
- 1 bell pepper
- 1 peach
- Large handful of blueberries
- ½ scallion
- 3 tablespoons hemp seeds
- 2 tablespoons balsamic vinegar
- Handful of sliced almonds
- Handful of fresh basil (minced)

Method:
1. Slice the courgette, either using a spiralizer or a julienne peeler (avoid the middle as it is not solid enough to make noodles)
2. Mince both the garlic and basil, and stir them into the courgette noodles
3. Stir in the balsamic vinegar
4. Chop the onion, pepper, peach, and tomato and stir them into the noodles
5. Stir in the almonds and hemp seed
6. Drizzle the olive oil and toss
7. Serve garnished with the blueberries

Tahini Courgette Noodles

This is another great courgette noodle dish with a good variety of vegetables in it, making it a nice summer dish with produce from your garden.

Ingredients:
- 1 yellow courgette (spiralized)
- 4 pieces of broccolini (tender stem broccoli) or purple sprouting broccoli (chopped)
- 4 leaves Romaine lettuce (chopped)
- 2 green onions (chopped)
- 1 carrot (shredded)
- 1 beet (shredded)
- ½ avocado (sliced)
- 1 teaspoon black sesame seeds

Dressing Ingredients:
- 2 tablespoons lemon juice
- 1 tablespoon tahini
- 1 teaspoon agave nectar or another liquid sweetener
- 1 teaspoon coconut aminos

Method:
1. Put all the vegetables into a bowl
2. In a separate bowl, mix together the dressing ingredients, whisking until smooth
3. Pour the dressing over the vegetables and garnish with sesame seeds

Rainbow Pad Thai

A lovely dish, full of nutrients and great to serve up to dinner guests. Use yellow courgette to give this some extra colour.

Ingredients:
- 1 medium courgette (spiralized)
- 1 medium orange carrot
- 1 medium purple carrot
- 1 medium yellow carrot
- 1½oz / 40g bell pepper (any colour, thinly sliced)
- ½ cup peanuts
- Several handfuls of bean sprouts

Sauce Ingredients:
- 2 garlic cloves (finely minced)
- 2 Kaffir lime leaves (thinly sliced)
- 2 tablespoons orange juice (fresh)
- 2 tablespoons sesame oil
- 2 tablespoons almond butter
- 1 tablespoon coconut sugar
- 2 teaspoons ginger (freshly minced)
- 2 teaspoons white miso
- 1 teaspoon coconut sugar
- ¼ teaspoon chilli flakes
- 1/3 cup water
- ¼ cup lime juice

Method:
1. Once peeled, slice the carrots lengthwise into thin ribbons, then cut into matchsticks
2. Put these vegetables into a large bowl
3. Blend all the sauce ingredients in your blender until smooth
4. Pour the sauce over the vegetables
5. Garnish with bean sprouts, chilli flakes, peanuts and lime wedges

Raw Courgette Chips

These are a great alternative to normal chips and are a surprisingly healthy alternative, being great for anyone on a diet.

Ingredients:

- 8 cups thinly sliced courgette (cut into rounds)
- ½ cup agave nectar
- ¼ cup extra-virgin olive oil
- ¼ cup balsamic vinegar
- 2 tablespoons each of dried basil, parsley, and oregano
- 1 tablespoons each of garlic and onion powder
- 1 teaspoon each of black pepper, crushed red pepper flakes, and salt

Method:

1. Pat dry the courgette after slicing it
2. Whisk together the rest of the ingredients in a small bowl
3. Pour the coating over the courgette and ensure the slices are well coated
4. Spread the courgette slices onto dehydrator sheets and dry at 145F for an hour before reducing the temperature to 120 and drying for a further 12 hours, until crispy (adjust drying times if using an oven)
5. Store in an airtight container and dehydrate for an extra few minutes to crisp them up again if necessary

Trio Pepper Salad
A simple dish, full of flavour and a great side dish for a meal or a picnic.

Ingredients:
- 3 bell peppers (one each of red, yellow and orange)
- 2 small courgettes
- ½ cup slivered raw almonds
- ½ lemon (juiced)
- Extra-virgin olive oil
- Salt and black pepper (to taste)
- Fresh herbs (to taste) such as basil, oregano or parsley

Method:
1. Cut both the courgette and pepper into thin, long strips and put to one side
2. Make a dressing by mixing the olive oil with the lemon juice and fresh herbs
3. Season to taste with salt and black pepper
4. Pour the dressing over the vegetables when ready to serve

Vegan Lasagne

This is a delicious raw lasagne that is dairy and gluten free and full of highly nutritious ingredients.

Pesto Ingredients:
- 3 cups raw spinach
- 1 head of broccoli (roughly chop the florets)
- 2/3 cup raw sunflower seeds (soaked overnight)
- 2 teaspoons extra-virgin online oil
- 2 teaspoons lemon juice
- Salt and pepper to taste

Sun-Dried Tomato Marinara Ingredients:
- 1 cup sun-dried tomatoes (soak for 30 minutes in hot water)
- 4 Medjool dates (soak for 10 minutes in hot water and remove the stone)
- 1 garlic clove (chopped)
- 1 tomato (cut in half)
- 2 tablespoons water
- 2 teaspoons fresh lemon juice
- 1 teaspoon no-salt seasoning

Cashew Cheese Ingredients:
- 1 cup raw cashew nuts (soaked overnight)
- 1 garlic clove (chopped)
- 2 teaspoons fresh lemon juice
- 1 teaspoon nutritional yeast
- 1 teaspoon herbs de Provence
- Salt and pepper to taste

Walnut Sausage Ingredients:
- 2 cups raw walnuts (soaked overnight)
- 2 tablespoons liquid aminos
- 1 teaspoon fresh rosemary (minced)
- 1 teaspoon each of fresh sage and thyme (minced)
- 1 teaspoon dried marjoram
- ½ teaspoon cayenne pepper
- ½ teaspoon dried thyme

Lasagne Ingredients:
- 2-4 large courgettes (thinly sliced lengthwise)

Sunflower Seed Pesto Method:
1. Rinse and strain the sunflower seeds
2. Put all of the ingredients into your food processor
3. Process until you get a pesto texture, i.e. Not too smooth or too rough
4. Season to taste with salt and pepper

Sun-Dried Tomato Marinara Method:
1. Drain the dates and tomatoes
2. Put everything into your food processor and process until it is blended but still chunky
3. Season to taste with salt and pepper

Cashew Cheese Method:
1. Drain and rinse the cashew nuts
2. Place all the ingredients into your food process
3. Blend, scraping down the sides until you get a ricotta cheese-like texture
4. Season to taste with salt and pepper

Walnut Sausage Method:
1. Add all of the ingredients to your food processor
2. Process until not quite smooth, but there are no large chunks of walnut left

Lasagne Method:
1. Put a layer of courgette slices down in your lasagne dish
2. Add a layer of pesto
3. Add another layer of courgette
4. Cover the courgette with the marinara sauce
5. Add another layer of courgette
6. Cover this with the cashew cheese
7. Add another layer of courgette
8. Add a layer of walnut sausage
9. Repeat as necessary until all of the ingredients are used up or make another lasagne in a separate dish
10. Serve garnished with microgreens or sprouts

Noodle Courgette Salad

A lovely dish that gets a slightly salty taste from the almond butter, but a delightful texture from the avocado. It's a very moreish dish and great during the summer months.

Ingredients:
- 1 courgette (spiralized)
- 1 cucumber (spiralized)
- ½ avocado (sliced)
- Handful of baby spinach leaves

Dressing Ingredients:
- 1 garlic clove (minced)
- 1 tablespoon extra-virgin olive oil
- 1 tablespoon almond butter
- Salt (to taste)

Method:
1. Mix the dressing ingredients in a small bowl, until thoroughly combined
2. Put the vegetables into a large bowl
3. Pour the dressing over the vegetables and stir well
4. Sprinkle with freshly ground salt and enjoy

Veggie Wraps
This is a great dish to make from the leftover vegetables found in your fridge, the leftovers from spiralizing courgette, the odd carrot or celery stick and so on. It's a good way to use up these leftovers and reduce waste in your kitchen.

Ingredients:
- 3 cups chopped vegetables (can be anything, courgette, carrots, peppers, celery, etc.)
- 2 cups water
- 1 cup flax meal
- 1 cup greens (e.g. Baby spinach – can be a combination of leftover greens)
- 2 tablespoons dry mixed herbs
- 1 teaspoon salt

Method:
1. Put the water, salt, greens, and vegetables into your food processor
2. Blend until it has a smooth and creamy texture
3. Pour out into a large bowl
4. Add the dry herbs and flax meal, mixing well
5. Stand for 15 to 20 minutes until thickened
6. Spread thinly onto silicone dehydrator sheets
7. Dehydrate for 1 hour at 115F/46C, then reduce the temperature for 105F/41C for a further 2 hours
8. Rotate the trays and continue to dehydrate for 1 to 2 hours, until dry, but still flexible

Courgette Hummus

Hummus is great when served with vegetable batons, crackers or pita bread. This is a simple recipe to make that has a delicious, creamy texture. Great to use as a snack.

Ingredients:

- 2 courgettes (chopped)
- 3 garlic cloves
- ¾ cup raw tahini
- ¾ cup brown sesame seeds (soak for 3 to 4 hours and rinse before use)
- ½ cup fresh lemon juice
- ¼ cup extra-virgin olive oil
- 1½ teaspoons paprika
- 1½ teaspoons Himalayan salt
- ¼ teaspoon cayenne powder

Method:

1. Put all of the ingredients, except the tahini and sesame seeds into your food processor
2. Blend until smooth
3. Scrape down the sides, add the tahini and sesame seeds
4. Continue to blend until smooth
5. Store in a glass jar for up to a week

BREADS, CAKES & BAKING

Courgettes can be used in a wide variety of baking. Just like you can make carrot cake, you can use courgette in your baking for a moist texture. Most people will not realize that you have used this vegetable in your baking, and this is a fantastic way to use up excess courgette and make them more appetizing to people.

Courgette Bread

This is a lovely bread that has a fine taste to it. It is moist and has a lovely texture, so is well worth trying with some spare courgettes.

Ingredients:

- 3 eggs
- 3 cups all-purpose (plain) flour
- 2¼ cups white (granulated) sugar
- 2 cups courgette (grated)
- 1 cup walnuts (chopped)
- 1 cup vegetable oil
- 1 tablespoon ground cinnamon
- 3 teaspoons vanilla extract
- 1 teaspoon baking powder
- 1 teaspoon baking soda
- 1 teaspoon salt

Method:

1. Grease two 8x4" pans and sprinkle with flour
2. Preheat your oven to 325F/165C
3. Sift into a large bowl the flour, baking powder, baking soda, cinnamon and salt
4. In a separate bowl, beat together the sugar, eggs, vanilla essence and vegetable oil
5. Add the dry ingredients to the wet, beating well
6. Stir in the walnuts and courgette until well combined but do not overmix
7. Pour this batter into the greased pans
8. Bake for between 40 and 60 minutes until a toothpick inserted into the middle of the bread comes out clean
9. Cool in the pan for around 20 minutes before removing the bread and cooling on a wire rack

Double Chocolate Bread

This is a really delicious bread that people will love to eat, not realizing that it contains courgette. Definitely worth a try and a very unusual use for courgette.

Ingredients:
- 2 large eggs
- 2 cups courgette (shredded and gently pressed down)
- 1 cup chocolate chips
- 1 2/3 cups all-purpose (plain) flour
- ½ cup vegetable oil
- ½ cup brown sugar
- 1/3 cup baking cocoa
- 1/3 cup honey
- 1 teaspoon vanilla extract
- 1 teaspoon salt
- ½ teaspoon baking powder
- ½ teaspoon baking soda
- ½ teaspoon espresso powder

Method:
1. Grease an 8x4" loaf pan
2. Preheat your oven to 350F/175C
3. In a large bowl, beat together the eggs, vanilla extract, sugar, vegetable oil and honey until it is smooth
4. Add the flour, cocoa powder, baking powder, baking soda and espresso powder and stir until thoroughly combined
5. Add the chocolate chips and courgette, stirring well
6. Pour into the prepared pan
7. Bake for 65-75 minutes, until a toothpick inserted into the middle of the cake comes out clean
8. Remove from the oven and cool for 10-15 minutes in the pan
9. Turn out onto a wire rack and allow to cool completed

Courgette Chocolate Cake

This is a surprising cake and, without a doubt, one of my favourite uses for courgettes. It works incredibly well, producing a moist, delicious cake that will have people coming back for seconds. The cake can then be covered with a chocolate glaze to make it even more appealing!

Ingredients:
- 2 large eggs
- 2½ cups all-purpose (plain) flour
- 2 cups courgette (grated)
- 1¾ cups sugar
- ¾ cup chocolate chips
- ½ cup butter
- ½ cup walnuts
- ½ cup buttermilk
- ½ cup vegetable oil
- ¼ cup cocoa
- 1 teaspoon salt
- 1 teaspoon vanilla extract
- 1 teaspoon baking soda

Method:
1. Grease a 9x13" pan and sprinkle with flour (substitute for a round pan if that is what you have to hand)
2. Preheat your oven to 325F/165C
3. Cream the butter in a large bowl
4. Add the sugar and vegetable oil, mixing well
5. Add the rest of the ingredients, except the walnuts and chocolate chips
6. Stir until well combined
7. Fold in the walnuts and chocolate chips
8. Pour into your pan
9. Bake for 50-60 minutes until a toothpick inserted into the middle of the cake comes out clean
10. Remove from the oven and cool

Courgette Brownies
These are delicious chocolate brownies with courgette in. Everyone will love these, and it's a great way to get children to eat up your excess courgette.

Ingredients:
- 10½oz / 300g caster (superfine) sugar
- 9oz / 250g courgette (grated)
- 9oz / 250g all-purpose (plain) flour
- 4½oz / 125ml vegetable oil
- 2oz / 60g walnuts (chopped)
- 1½oz / 40g cocoa powder
- 2 teaspoons vanilla extract
- 1½ teaspoons baking soda (bicarbonate of soda)
- 1 teaspoon salt

Icing Ingredients:
- 9oz / 250g icing (confectioners') sugar
- 6 tablespoons cocoa powder
- 4 tablespoons milk
- 4 tablespoons butter
- ½ teaspoons vanilla extract

Method:
1. Grease a 9x13" baking tin and sprinkle with flour
2. Preheat your oven to 355F/180C
3. In a large bowl, stir together the vegetable oil, sugar and two teaspoons of vanilla extract until thoroughly combined
4. In a separate bowl, mix together the flour, cocoa powder, salt and baking soda
5. Add this to the sugar mixture and stir well
6. Fold in the walnuts and courgette
7. Spread into the prepared baking tin
8. Bake for around 30 minutes until the brownies spring back when you push down gently on them
9. Remove from the oven and allow to cool in the pan before turning out onto a wire rack
10. Melt the butter and cocoa powder together and leave to cool
11. In another bowl, mix the milk with the confectioners' sugar and vanilla extract
12. Add the cocoa/butter mixture and stir until well combined

13. Coat the cooled brownies with icing then cut to size

Carrot and Courgette Muffins

These are great muffins made from two surprisingly versatile vegetables. These are very light and moist, and will soon become a firm favourite.

Ingredients:
- 3 eggs (lightly beaten)
- 2 cups carrots (shredded)
- 2 cups all-purpose (plain) flour
- 1¼ cups sugar
- 1 cup courgette (shredded)
- 1 cup apple (peeled and chopped)
- ¾ cup vegetable oil
- ¾ cup flaked coconut
- ½ cup almonds (chopped)
- 1 tablespoon ground cinnamon
- 2 teaspoons baking soda
- 2 teaspoons orange zest
- 1 teaspoon vanilla extract
- ½ teaspoon salt

Method:
1. Preheat your oven to 375F/190C
2. In a large bowl, mix together the apple, courgette, carrot, orange peel and almonds, then put to one side
3. In a separate large bowl, mix together the flour, sugar, salt, baking soda, and cinnamon
4. In a small bowl, mix together the vegetable oil, vanilla extract, and eggs
5. Add the wet ingredients to the flour mixture and stir in until just combined
6. Gently fold in the carrot and courgette mixture
7. Fill paper muffin cups about two-thirds full with the mixture
8. Bake for 20-22 minutes until a toothpick inserted into the middle comes out clean
9. Cool in the muffin tin for 10 minutes, then remove and place on a wire rack to finish cooling

Courgette Chocolate Chip Cookies

Another great way to use up your courgette, few people will realize there is a vegetable hiding in these cookies, and they will quickly get eaten.

Ingredients:
- 1 large egg
- 1 2/3 cups chocolate chips (dark or milk)
- 1½ cups courgette (shredded)
- 1½ cups all-purpose (plain) flour
- 1 cup quick oats
- 1 cup mixed nuts (chopped)
- 2/3 cup white (granulated) sugar
- ½ cup butter (softened)
- 1 teaspoon ground cinnamon
- ¾ teaspoon vanilla extract
- ½ teaspoon baking soda

Method:
1. Preheat your oven to 350F/175C
2. Lightly grease some baking sheets
3. In a small bowl, mix together the flour, baking soda, and cinnamon
4. In a large bowl, use a mixer to beat the sugar and butter together
5. Add the vanilla extract and the egg, and beat thoroughly
6. Add the courgette and mix again
7. Gradually beat in the flour mixture
8. Stir in the nuts, chocolate chips, and the oats until just combined
9. Drop rounded teaspoons of this mixture onto the greased baking sheets about 2" apart
10. Bake for around 10 minutes, until they are a light golden brown colour at the edges
11. Cool for 2 minutes on the baking sheet before removing to cool on a wire rack

Nutty Chocolate Chip Cookies

These are great cookies that go down well. Substitute hazelnut, macadamia or pecan for walnuts if you prefer for a different taste. This will make a lot of cookies, somewhere around 90, depending on how you make them. Half the recipe to make about 45 cookies if you prefer.

Ingredients:
- 2 eggs (beaten)
- 4 cups all-purpose (plain) flour
- 2 cups courgette (grated)
- 2 cups white (granulated) sugar
- 2 cups chocolate chips
- 1½ cups walnuts (chopped)
- 1 cup butter (softened)
- 2 teaspoons ground cinnamon
- 2 teaspoons baking soda
- 1 teaspoon salt

Method:
1. Preheat your oven to 350F/175C
2. Grease your cookie sheets
3. Cream the sugar and butter in a large bowl, use an electric mixer as it is easier and quicker
4. In a small bowl, mix together the flour, cinnamon, salt and baking soda
5. Mix the egg into the creamed butter and sugar
6. Gradually mix in the flour mixture
7. Stir in, by hand, the courgette
8. Carefully fold in the chocolate chips and walnuts
9. Drop rounded teaspoons of the mixture onto the cookie sheets about 2" apart
10. Bake for between 15 and 20 minutes until golden brown, being careful not to over cook
11. Leave to stand on the cookie sheet for 2-3 minutes before removing the cookies from the tray and cooking on a wire rack

Courgette Bread

A lovely, fluffy bread that is surprisingly healthy with whole grades, coconut oil and maple syrup in it. As a moist bread, it will only last for a couple of days at room temperature. It will store in your refrigerator for up to a week and freezes for up to three months.

Ingredients:
- 2 eggs
- 1¾ cup whole wheat flour
- 1½ cups courgette (grated – squeeze out moisture first)
- ¾ cup walnuts or pecans (roughly chopped)
- ½ cup milk (any type) or water
- ½ cup maple syrup or honey
- 1/3 cup coconut oil (melted) or extra-virgin olive oil
- 2 teaspoons vanilla extract
- 1 teaspoon baking soda
- 1 teaspoon ground cinnamon (plus extra for decoration)
- ½ teaspoon salt
- ¼ teaspoon ground nutmeg

Method:
- Preheat your oven to 325F/165C
- Grease a 9x5" loaf pan
- Toast the nuts on a lined baking sheet for about 5 minutes, until fragrant, stirring halfway through cooking then leave to one side to cool
- In a large bowl, mix together the honey and coconut oil, beating with a whisk until well combined
- Add the eggs and continue to beat (note the coconut oil can solidify when cold ingredients are added in which case microwave for 10-20 seconds or leave in a warm place for a few minutes to allow it to melt)
- Add the nutmeg, salt, vanilla extract, baking soda, milk, and cinnamon, whisking well until thoroughly combined
- Gently stir in the courgette
- Add the flour and stir until just combined, don't worry if the mixture is lumpy
- Fold in the toasted nuts
- Pour the batter into the greased loaf pan and sprinkle with ground cinnamon

- Back for between 55 and 60 minutes until a toothpick inserted into the middle comes out clean
- Leave to cool in the loaf pan for ten minutes before turning out onto a wire rack to finish cooling

Alternative Courgette Bread

This is a different recipe for courgette bread that has a very interesting taste. This is well worth a try as it is unusual and very tasty.

Ingredients:

- 4 eggs
- 1 ripe banana (mashed)
- 1 cup courgette (shredded and squeezed to remove excess moisture)
- ½ cup coconut flour
- ½ cup walnuts
- 2-3 tablespoons maple syrup or raw honey (to taste)
- 1 tablespoon ground cinnamon
- 1 tablespoon coconut oil
- 1 teaspoon apple cider vinegar
- ¾ teaspoon baking soda
- ½ teaspoon salt
- ½ teaspoon ground nutmeg

Method:

1. Preheat your oven to 350F/175C
2. Grease a small loaf pan (use coconut oil)
3. In a large bowl, mix together the coconut oil, honey, egg, and banana
4. Mix in all of the dry ingredients and the courgette, until well combined
5. Add the apple cider vinegar and stir until smooth
6. Fold in the nuts
7. Pour into your loaf pan and bake for 45-50 minutes until a toothpick inserted into the middle comes out clean
8. Cool for 10 minutes in the pan before turning out onto a wire rack to finish cooling

SOUP RECIPES

Courgette is a great ingredient for soups, whether as the main component or as a complimentary ingredient. Any type of courgette can be used in soups, from yellow to green to round.

All of these soups can be frozen, but do not add any milk, cheese or fresh herbs before you freeze the soup. These are added when you defrost the soup and reheat it, just before serving.

Cream of Courgette Soup

A simple to make soup that can be made entirely of home grown ingredients.

Ingredients:

- 32oz chicken or vegetable stock
- 3 medium courgettes (top and tailed and cut into chunks)
- 2 garlic cloves
- ½ small onion (quartered)
- 2 tablespoons sour cream (you can use a reduced fat version)
- Salt and pepper to taste
- Grated Parmesan cheese to garnish (optional)

Method:

1. Put the stock, onion, courgette, and garlic in a large pot
2. Heat over a medium heat until it boils
3. Reduce the heat, cover and simmer for approximately 20 minutes until tender
4. Remove from the heat
5. Purée with a stick blender
6. Add the sour cream, then purée again until smooth
7. Season to taste, return to heat but do not boil
8. Serve hot garnished with grated Parmesan

Thai Curry Courgette Soup

This is a tasty soup with a good mix of flavours that goes down well. Optionally, you can add a teaspoon of fish sauce for extra flavour, but this can be left out to make this soup vegetarian. It is best served hot, garnished with fresh cilantro (coriander).

Ingredients:
- 3 garlic cloves (diced)
- 2 medium courgettes (diced)
- 1 large brown onion (diced)
- 1 cup coconut milk (shake the can well before pouring)
- 1 cup vegetable stock
- 2 tablespoons fresh lime juice
- 1 tablespoon ghee or coconut oil
- 2 teaspoons turmeric powder
- 1 teaspoon mild curry powder
- ½ teaspoon sea salt
- ¼ teaspoon white or black pepper

Method:
1. Heat the ghee or coconut oil in a saucepan over a medium heat
2. Sauté the onion for 5 minutes, stirring, until golden and softened
3. Add the garlic, courgette, and salt, stirring well
4. Add the curry powder, pepper, and turmeric, stirring well
5. Add the vegetable stock, coconut milk and fish sauce (if using), stirring until well combined
6. Bring to the boil then reduce the heat, cover a simmer for 10 minutes
7. Add the lime juice, stir well and serve garnished with fresh cilantro

Courgette and Potato Soup

This is a great soup to make from your home-made produce. As many people will grow both potatoes and courgette, use any variety that you have to hand of both the vegetables.

Ingredients:

- 8 courgettes (peeled and diced)
- 2 potatoes (peeled and diced)
- 2 onions (chopped)
- 34fl oz / 1¾ pints / 1 litre vegetable or chicken stock
- ½ pint / 250ml full-fat milk
- 1oz / 30g butter
- 4 tablespoons instant mash potato flakes
- 4 tablespoons fresh dill (chopped)
- 1 tablespoon soy sauce
- ½ teaspoon dried basil
- ¼ teaspoon each dried thyme, dried rosemary and ground white pepper

Method:

1. In a large frying pan or wok, melt the butter and sauté the onions until translucent
2. Add the potatoes courgette, basil, rosemary, thyme and white pepper
3. Cook, stirring often, for 5 minutes
4. Bring the stock to the boil in a large saucepan
5. Add the vegetable mixture, reduce the heat and simmer for about 15 minutes until all the vegetables are tender
6. Liquidize then return to the saucepan
7. Add the milk, bring close to boiling point, but do not boil
8. Add the mash potato granules and soy sauce, stirring well
9. Season to taste
10. Serve hot or chilled, garnished with dill

Carrot and Courgette Soup

Another great home-made soup that can be made from vegetables grown in your garden. Definitely worth a try and can be made some intriguing colours through the use of coloured courgette and carrots!

Ingredients:
- 1 pint / 600ml vegetable or chicken stock
- ½lb / 225g courgette (topped and tailed and sliced)
- ½lb / 225g carrots (peeled and sliced)
- 2oz / 50g butter
- 1 bay leaf
- 1½ tablespoons sugar
- 1 tablespoon tomato puree
- ½ teaspoon fresh coriander
- Salt and pepper to taste

Method:
1. Melt the butter in a large saucepan and cook the courgette and carrots, covered, on a low heat for 10 minutes, until soft
2. Add the rest of the ingredients and simmer for a further 30 minutes
3. Remove the bay leaf and then purée the soup
4. Season to taste and serve

Creamy Courgette Soup

This is a very tasty soup and, again, many of the ingredients can be grown at home. Use baby spinach leaves if you can, though if the spinach in your garden has gone beyond its best, you can still use older leaves. You may need to adjust the cooking time slightly as they can be tougher.

Ingredients:

- 34fl oz / 1¾ pints / 1 litre vegetable or chicken stock
- 8fl oz / 1 cup / 225ml cream
- 1 onion (roughly chopped)
- 1 potato (diced)
- 1lb / 500g courgette (diced)
- 5¼oz /150g spinach
- 2 tablespoons vegetable oil
- 1 tablespoon fresh parsley (finely chopped)
- Salt and pepper to taste

Method:

1. Heat the oil in a large saucepan and sauté the onion and courgette until the onion becomes translucent
2. Add everything except the cream and simmer for a further 20-25 minutes until the vegetables are soft
3. Purée the soup
4. Stir in the cream and warm
5. Season to taste and serve

Fennel and Courgette Soup

Fennel is a vegetable few people grow at home because it doesn't get on well with many other plants and takes a long time to mature. However, it works really well in this soup, giving it a fantastic flavour.

Ingredients:
- 1 courgette (thinly sliced)
- 1 fennel bulb (diced) – retain the green leaves and use, chopped, as a garnish
- 1 onion (finely chopped)
- 1 pint / 500ml vegetable of chicken stock
- 2 tablespoons butter
- 1 teaspoon mild curry powder
- Dash of white wine vinegar
- Salt and pepper to taste

Method:
1. Heat the butter in a large saucepan and sauté the onion until soft
2. Add the courgette and fennel, cooking for a further 3 minutes, stirring often
3. Add the stock, cover and simmer on a low heat for 10 to 15 minutes until the fennel has softened
4. Purée the soup, adding more water/stock until you get the desired consistency
5. Season to taste
6. Add the curry powder and white wine vinegar, stirring well
7. Serve hot, garnished with chopped fennel greens

Tomato and Courgette Soup

A great dish that has a wonderful, full taste. Use heritage tomatoes for improved flavour or to add colour to this soup.

Ingredients:

- 1lb / 500g courgette (sliced)
- 2 garlic cloves (finely chopped)
- 2 onions (roughly chopped)
- 1 large tomato (chopped)
- 34fl oz / 1¾ pints / 1 litre vegetable or chicken stock
- 2 tablespoons vegetable oil
- 2 teaspoons fresh lemon juice
- 2 teaspoons salt
- ½ teaspoon each of dried oregano, basil, parsley
- ½ teaspoon caster (superfine) sugar
- ¼ teaspoon ground nutmeg
- ¼ teaspoon hot pepper sauce
- ¼ teaspoon Worcestershire sauce
- Salt and pepper to taste

Method:

1. Put the courgette into a colander and sprinkle with salt, leaving for half an hour before draining and patting dry
2. Heat the oil in a large pot over a medium heat
3. Sauté the garlic, onions, and courgette for about ten minutes until the onions become translucent
4. Add the tomato and stock, reducing the heat and simmering for 20 minutes
5. Using a slotted spoon, remove the vegetables from the stock and purée them, returning them back to the pan afterward
6. Stir in the rest of the ingredients, season to taste and simmer for a further 5 minutes before serving

Spicy Thai Courgette Soup

This is a soup that has a bit of bite to it, but not in an unpleasant way. Feel free to adjust the amount and heat of the curry paste to your personal preference.

Ingredients:
- 1 onion (finely chopped)
- ½lb / 250g courgette (grated)
- ½lb / 250g sweet potato (grated)
- 2½ pints / 1½ litres vegetable or chicken stock
- ½ pint / 250ml coconut milk
- 1 tablespoon Thai curry paste
- Extra-virgin olive oil for frying

Method:
1. Heat the oil in a large saucepan over a medium heat and sauté the onion until soft
2. Add the curry paste and stir until the fragrance is released
3. Add the sweet potato, courgette, and stock
4. Bring to the boil, stirring occasionally then reduce the heat and simmer for a further 30 minutes until soft
5. Remove from the heat and stir in the coconut milk
6. Purée until smooth
7. Reheat and serve hot, garnished with mint or cilantro (coriander) leaves

Brie and Courgette Soup

A very unusual soup that is bound to impress anyone you serve it to. It has a very full flavour and is really delicious.

Ingredients:
- 21oz / 600g courgette (chopped)
- 9oz / 250g onion (finely chopped)
- 8oz / 225g potato (peeled and diced)
- 8oz / 225g Brie cheese (with extra to garnish)
- 1oz / 25g butter
- 15 basil leaves (torn)
- 1 garlic clove (finely chopped)
- ½ pint / 300ml vegetable stock
- 7fl oz / 200ml milk
- 3 tablespoons double cream
- Splash of white wine

Method:
1. In a large saucepan, melt the butter and sauté the onion for a few minutes until softened
2. Add the white wine, garlic, and potato, cooking for another 5 minutes
3. Stir in the courgette and vegetable stock and bring to the boil
4. Reduce the heat, cover and simmer on a low heat until the potatoes are cooked through, about 20-25 minutes
5. Add the milk and Brie, heating through until the cheese has melted
6. Add the basil and cream, stirring well, ensuring it doesn't boil
7. Season to taste, serving topped with Brie slices and torn basil

Pea, Mint and Courgette Soup

An unusual soup that is very nice and worth a try. It is one that most people will not be familiar with so should be tried at least once. This soup can be served hot or chilled, depending on your preference.

Ingredients:

- 3 medium courgettes (grated)
- 1 onion (diced)
- 1½ pints / 1 ½ litres vegetable (or chicken) stock
- 10½oz / 300g peas (frozen)
- 2 teaspoons mint leaves (fresh)
- 6 tablespoons crème fraîche
- 1 teaspoon butter

Method:

1. Heat the butter in a large saucepan and sauté the onion until soft
2. Add the peas and courgette, stirring so they are coated with butter
3. Add the stock then boil until the peas are tender
4. Reduce the heat to a simmer and add the mint and crème fraîche
5. Blend until it reaches your preferred consistency

Coriander and Courgette Soup

A nice soup with a hint of spice from the coriander (cilantro).

Ingredients:

- 2.2lb / 1kg courgette (diced)
- 1 large potato (diced)
- 2 garlic cloves (chopped)
- ½ shallot (diced)
- 1oz / 25g fresh chopped cilantro (coriander)
- 1 tablespoon crème fraîche
- Salt and pepper to taste

Method:

1. Put all the ingredients, except the crème fraîche in a large saucepan
2. Cover with water and bring to the boil,
3. Cover, reduce the heat and cook until all the vegetables are tender
4. Purée the soup to your preferred consistency
5. Return to the heat, stir in the crème fraîche and serve hot

CHUTNEYS & PRESERVES

Courgette works particularly well in a chutney, and as chutneys store for up to a year, this is an ideal way for you to store your courgette for use through the colder months. Chutneys originated in India and were brought back to Europe by British explorers. They have since been wholeheartedly adopted and turned into an entire industry in the United Kingdom and are gradually spreading further afield in their popularity.

Chutney is made from a wide variety of ingredients, though usually involving onions and vinegar, which acts as a preservative. All chutneys are best left for several weeks, if not a few months for the flavour to develop fully, depending on the amount and type of vinegar in the recipe.

Most chutneys will work well with cheese or cold meat. It is fantastic in a sandwich with cheese or ham or even both and can liven up a boring tasting sandwich, giving it a bit of a tang. Many work well on the side too, and they can be added to dishes such as spaghetti Bolognese to give it a little something special.

Sweet Courgette Chutney

This is delicious chutney that has more of a relish consistency. This chutney will store for two to three months in normal jars but will benefit from going through a canning process for it to last longer due to the low levels of the preserving vinegar used. This recipe makes enough for seven 1 pint jars.

Ingredients:
- 12 cups courgette (shredded)
- 6 cups white (granulated) sugar
- 4 cups onion (chopped)
- 2½ cups white vinegar
- 1 green bell pepper (finely chopped)
- 1 red bell pepper (finely chopped)
- 5 tablespoons canning salt
- 1 tablespoon corn-starch
- 1½ teaspoons celery seed
- ¾ teaspoon ground turmeric
- ¾ teaspoon ground nutmeg
- ½ teaspoon ground black pepper

Method:
1. Put the onion and courgette into a large, non-metallic bowl
2. Add the salt and mix well, using your hands, until all the vegetables are covered in it
3. Cover, then refrigerate overnight
4. Drain the liquid from the courgette and rinse well with cold water
5. Squeeze out any excess moisture and pat dry, putting the onion and courgette to one side
6. Add everything into a large pot and stir well, ensuring it is well mixed
7. Bring to the boil, then reduce the heat and simmer on a medium to low heat for 30 minutes
8. Fill the jars and process in your canner immediately

Simple Courgette Chutney

A wonderfully simple chutney that makes enough for a month or two of use. Unlike many other chutneys, this must be kept refrigerated due to the low vinegar content.

Ingredients:
- 2.2lb / 1kg courgette (chopped into small pieces)
- 9oz / 250g dark brown soft sugar
- 1 onion (finely chopped)
- 1 green bell pepper (finely chopped)
- 1 garlic clove (minced)
- 1 apple (tart – peeled, cored and finely chopped)
- 1 cup / 250ml white wine vinegar
- 1 tablespoon English mustard
- 1 tablespoon fresh ginger (grated)
- ½ teaspoon salt
- ¼ teaspoon crushed red chilli flakes

Method:
1. Put all the ingredients into a large saucepan
2. Bring to the boil, stirring occasionally
3. Reduce the heat and simmer for 45 to 55 minutes until thickened
4. Cool, jar and refrigerate

Spicy Courgette Chutney

This chutney works well with cold meats and cheese, being delicious in sandwiches. This can be stored for up to a year in sterilized jars in a cool, dark place. Cut the vegetables to the same size to ensure even cooking, but don't cut them too small otherwise they will break down into mush.

Ingredients:
- 4 medium courgettes (diced)
- 3 medium cooking apples (peeled, cored and diced)
- 3 medium onions (diced)
- 14oz / 400g light, soft brown sugar
- 7oz / 200g sultanas
- 1oz / 25g fresh ginger (grated)
- 1½ cups / 400ml apple cider vinegar
- 1-2 teaspoons dried chilli flakes (to taste)
- 1 teaspoon salt

Spice Bag Ingredients:
- 2 teaspoons black peppercorns
- 2 teaspoons coriander seeds
- 2 teaspoons mustard seeds

Method:
1. Put the spice bag ingredients into a small muslin bag and tie it
2. Add all of the ingredients, except the sugar, to a large saucepan, including the spice bag
3. Stir well then cover and bring to the boil slowly
4. Reduce the heat and simmer for half an hour
5. Remove the lid and remove from the heat
6. Stir in the sugar, ensuring it is dissolved
7. Return to a low heat and simmer for between 1½ and 2 hours, stirring occasionally
8. When the liquid has reduced and the courgette looks plump, then jar

Tasty Courgette Relish

This is a great relish that takes a little while to make but is certainly worth the effort. This will store for several months, though refrigerate once opened. Once cooled, this can be stored in your freezer, being defrosted as required.

Day 1 Ingredients:
- 10 cups courgette (finely diced)
- 4 cups onions (finely diced)
- 5 tablespoons salt

Day 2 Ingredients:
- 3½ cups white (granulated) sugar
- 2 cups white vinegar
- 4 tablespoons corn-starch (mixed with cold water)
- 2 tablespoons celery seeds
- 1 tablespoon English mustard powder
- 1 teaspoon ground turmeric

Method:
1. Mix the courgette and onion in a large bowl with the salt, ensuring it is thoroughly combined
2. Cover with plastic wrap and put to one side overnight
3. The next day, rinse in a sieve until the salt has been rinsed off
4. Add all of the ingredients to a large saucepan, and stir well
5. Cook, stirring often, on a medium to high heat, for 30 minutes, adding water as required
6. When the courgette is soft, but before it breaks down, remove from the heat and jar

Ginger Courgette Chutney

This chutney is a fantastic combination of tart apples and spices that makes for a delicious treat. Leave for at least a week before using and store in a cool dark place for up to a year. Once opened, refrigerate. Make sure all of the vegetables are cut to about the same size to ensure everything cooks evening. Use this within 3 months.

Ingredients:
- 8 cups courgette (diced)
- 4 cups onion (diced)
- 2 cups tart apple (cored, not peeled and diced)
- 2 cups apple cider vinegar
- 1 cup raisins
- 1½ cups brown sugar (packed)
- ¼ cup / 60ml lemon juice
- 4 garlic cloves (minced)
- 3 tablespoons fresh ginger (grated)
- 2 tablespoons ground coriander
- 2 teaspoons garam masala
- 1 teaspoon ground cumin
- 1 teaspoon ground cayenne pepper

Method:
1. Put everything into a large saucepan and bring to the boil
2. Reduce the heat and simmer, stirring occasionally, until the vegetables are tender and the liquid has thickened, about 2 hours. Remember the liquid will thicken further as it cools
3. Jar while hot and seal immediately. You can process this in a canner for longer term storage.

Spicy Tomato Chutney
A delicious chutney that has a wonderful spicy flavour. This works very well with a ploughman's lunch. Leave for about three weeks to mature before using.

Ingredients:
- 2 garlic cloves (crushed and finely chopped)
- 2 green cardamoms (seeds only)
- 1 cinnamon stick (broken in half)
- 3 whole cloves
- 9oz / 250g cherry tomatoes (cut into eighths)
- 9oz / 250g courgette (finely chopped)
- 4¼oz / 120g light brown muscovado sugar
- 3½oz / 100g apple (cored, peeled and diced)
- 3½oz / 100g sultanas
- ½oz / 10g fresh ginger root (grated)
- 5fl oz / ½ cup /150ml apple cider vinegar
- 1 teaspoon yellow mustard seeds
- 1 teaspoon black mustard seeds
- ¼ teaspoon whole coriander (cilantro) seeds
- ¼ teaspoon fennel seeds
- Fresh nutmeg (grated)

Method:
1. Using a pestle and mortar, grind together the cardamom seeds coriander seeds, fennel seeds and nutmeg to make a coarse powder
2. Put all of the ingredients, including the spices, into a large pan
3. Stir until well combined, then bring to the boil
4. Reduce the heat and simmer for an hour until thickened
5. Jar and seal while hot

Runner Bean and Courgette Chutney

A very interesting chutney that uses two ingredients many of us have in abundance in our gardens. Allow to mature for a month before using and store in a cool dark place for up to a year. Once opened, keep refrigerated.

Ingredients:
- 4 courgettes (thinly sliced)
- 2 onions (finely chopped)
- 21oz / 600g runner beans (thinly sliced)
- 16oz / 450g light, soft brown sugar
- 12oz / 350g cooking apples (peeled, cored and chopped)
- 2½ cups / 600ml cider vinegar
- 1 teaspoon coriander seeds
- 1 teaspoon ground turmeric
- 1 teaspoon English mustard powder

Method:
1. Put all of the ingredients into a large saucepan and stir well, ensuring they are thoroughly combined
2. Cook on a low heat, stirring constantly until the sugar has dissolved completely
3. Bring to the boil and cook on a rolling boil for 10 minutes, stirring occasionally
4. Reduce the heat and simmer for a further 1½ hours, stirring occasionally and stirring more frequently as the mixture thickens to prevent it sticking
5. Put all of the ingredients into a large pan and stir well, ensuring thoroughly combined
6. Cook on a gentle heat, stirring continuously until the sugar has dissolved
7. Bring to the boil and then simmer on a rolling boil for around 10 minutes, stirring occasionally
8. Reduce to a low simmer and cook, stirring regularly for about 90 minutes until the vegetables are tender and the mixture has thickened. You will need to stir the chutney more frequently towards the end of the cooking time to prevent it from sticking to the pan
9. Jar and store

Apricot Courgette Chutney

This is an unusual combination of flavours that work very well together in this chutney. Leave for six weeks, if you can, for the flavours to mature before using and serve with cheese, cold meats, breads and in sandwiches.

Ingredients:

- 10½oz / 300g courgette (diced)
- 9oz / 250g dried apricots (diced)
- 9oz / 250g cooking apples (peeled, cored and diced)
- 9oz / 250g white (granulated) sugar
- 8oz / 225g red onions (peeled and diced)
- 1¼ cups / 300ml distilled white malt vinegar
- 1 teaspoon ground ginger
- ½ teaspoon salt
- ½ teaspoon ground allspice

Method:

1. Put all the ingredients into a large saucepan and stir well
2. Heat, stirring continuously, on a medium heat until the sugar has completely dissolved
3. Bring to the boil then reduce the heat and simmer at a rolling boil for 40 to 45 minutes, stirring often until the right consistency is achieved
4. Jar and store

Courgette Pickle

This is a sharp pickle that works well in sandwiches, burgers and is particularly good with cold poached salmon. This pickle will store for a couple of months in your refrigerator and is best left for a few days to mature before use.

Ingredients:

- 3 shallots (finely chopped)
- 500g courgette (thinly sliced)
- 2 tablespoons salt

Pickling Vinegar Ingredients:

- 500ml cider vinegar
- 140g golden superfine (caster) sugar
- ½ dried chilli (crumbled)
- 1 teaspoon ground turmeric
- 1 teaspoon mustard seeds
- 1 teaspoon celery seeds
- 1 teaspoon English mustard powder

Method:

1. Put the courgette and shallots in a bowl, add the salt and cover with cold water
2. Stir and leave for 1 hour
3. Drain the liquid and pat dry
4. Put the pickling vinegar ingredients in a large pan and simmer for 3 to 5 minutes, stirring often, until the sugar has dissolved
5. Allow to cool so the liquid is warm, not hot
6. Add the courgette and shallots, stirring well
7. Jar and store in your refrigerator

Lemony Courgette Relish

An unusual relish with a definite Middle Eastern flavour to it. This relish works well with chicken and in sandwiches. Refrigerate and use within a month.

Ingredients:

- 6 medium courgettes (shredded)
- 1 large lemon
- 1½ cups golden raisins
- 1½ cups yellow onion (chopped)
- 1 cup white wine
- ¾ cup honey
- ¾ cup fresh lemon juice
- ¼ cup white (granulated) sugar
- 1 teaspoon salt

Method:

1. Put the courgette into a colander and sprinkle the salt over it, stirring well
2. Leave for 30 minutes and drain
3. Squeeze the courgette dry in paper until it is just about moist
4. Remove the rind from the lemon, careful not to get any white pith
5. Put the rind in a small saucepan, cover with water and bring to the boil
6. Simmer until the rind is tender, around 15 minutes
7. Drain, cool and then finely chop the rind
8. Put everything into a large saucepan and bring to the boil, stirring occasionally
9. Reduce the heat and simmer for around 35 minutes until thickened
10. Cool and store in airtight containers

Courgette Jam

This is a variation on the chutney, though is sweeter, making it great for sandwiches, particularly with cheese or cold meats. It will store for several months and is best kept in your refrigerator.

Ingredients:

- 8 cups courgette (peeled, de-seeded and pureed)
- 6 cups white (granulated) sugar
- 1 cup lemon juice
- 2 x 6oz packs of raspberry Jell-O gelatine
- 1 x 1¾oz pack of pectin

Method:

1. Put the lemon juice and courgette into a large saucepan
2. Bring to a rolling boil and cook, stirring occasionally, for 15 minutes
3. Add the rest of the ingredients and stir continuously until dissolved
4. Boil for a further 10 minutes, stirring occasionally
5. Jar and seal

Pineapple Courgette Jam

This is a lovely sweet jam, the pineapple giving this a wonderful taste. This will last in your refrigerator for about three weeks.

Ingredients:
- 6 cups courgette (de-seeded, peeled and shredded)
- 6 cups white (granulated) sugar
- ½ cup lemon juice
- 20oz can crushed pineapple (do not drain)
- 1 x 6oz pack of strawberry gelatine

Method:
1. Put the sugar and courgette in a large saucepan and bring to the boil
2. Boil, stirring continuously, for 6 minutes
3. Add the pineapple and lemon juice, reduce the heat slightly and cook for a further 8 minutes, stirring regularly
4. Add the gelatine and cook for a further minute, stirring continuously
5. Remove from the heat and skim off any foam
6. Jar, cool then seal

Courgette Marmalade

This is a great variation on marmalade that makes good use of courgette. This is delicious on toast and a must for anyone who likes marmalade. This will last up to 6 weeks in your refrigerator.

Ingredients:

- 7 cups white (granulated) sugar
- 4 cups courgette (grated – do not peel, remove any large seeds)
- 1½ cups orange sections
- ¾ cup lemon juice
- 1 medium lemon
- 2 x Certo liquid pectin pouches (1½oz per pouch)

Method:

1. Put the orange sections and courgette in a large saucepan
2. Remove the rind from the lemon and scrape off (discarding) around half of the white pith
3. Finely slice the rind and cut the lemon into sections before chopping it
4. Add the chopped lemon, rind and lemon juice to the courgette mixture
5. Add the sugar and stir until thoroughly combined
6. Using a high heat, bring the pan to a rolling boil for one minute, stirring all the time
7. Remove from the heat and stir in the liquid pectin
8. Stir for 7 minutes, skimming off any foam, making sure the fruit does not float
9. Pour into jars, filling to ¼" from the rim and seal while still hot

Pickled Courgette

These make for a great alternative to regular pickles, and you can adjust the spices according to your personal tastes. This recipe can be stored in regular screw top jars where it will last for a couple of months in your refrigerator or can be canned, in which case it will last a year or more.

Ingredients:

- 2lb courgettes (thinly sliced)
- ½lb onions (quartered then sliced thinly)
- 2 cups white (granulated) sugar
- ¼ cup salt
- 2 teaspoons mustard seeds
- 1 teaspoon ground turmeric
- 1 teaspoon celery seed
- 1 teaspoon prepared yellow mustard

Method:

1. Put the onions and courgette into a large bowl
2. Cover them with water, add the salt and stir well
3. Leave for a minimum of 2 hours before draining and putting in a large heatproof bowl
4. Add the rest of the ingredients to a large saucepan and bring to the boil
5. Remove from the heat and pour over the courgette
6. Stir well and leave to stand for 2 hours
7. Put the mixture into a large saucepan and boil for 3 minutes
8. Jar and seal or process in your canner

Courgette Dill Pickles

These are another great variation on the traditional pickles, though this recipe has a bit more of a kick than the previous one. Cut the courgette into spears or rounds, like traditional dill pickles. As with the previous recipe, you can jar and store in your refrigerator, or you can process these in a canner for a longer lifespan. If you are storing in your refrigerator, then you may want to half the recipe. Use in the same way as you would use dill pickles, such as on sandwiches and in burgers.

Ingredients:
- 2lb courgette (cut to shape)
- 2½ cups white wine vinegar
- ¼ cup white (granulated) sugar)
- 12 fresh dill sprigs
- 4 red jalapeño chillies (split lengthwise)
- 4 garlic cloves (halved)
- 4 tablespoons sea salt (divided)
- 2 teaspoons brown or yellow mustard seeds
- 1 teaspoon dill seeds
- 1 teaspoon coriander seeds
- ¼ teaspoon saffron threads

Method:
1. Put the cut courgette into a large bowl
2. Add 4 cups of ice, and 2 tablespoons of salt then cover with cold water
3. Put a plate on top to keep the courgette under the water
4. Leave for two hours before draining and rinsing
5. Put two clean, sterilized 1-quart jars on the side; they should be hot
6. Divide the dill, chillies, garlic and spices evenly between the two jars
7. Put the vinegar, sugar, 2 tablespoons of salt and 1¼ cups of water into a large saucepan and boil
8. In batches, cook the courgette in this liquid until it turns a khaki green colour and pliable, which should be around 2 minutes
9. Transfer the cooked courgette to the jars
10. When all the courgette has been cooked, pour the hot vinegar into the jars, leaving about ½" headspace
11. Jar and seal or can

SNACK RECIPES

Courgette makes for a great snack, and there are lots of delicious recipes you could make with them. Here are some of the best snack recipes for courgettes. These can also be served as a side dish to a main course or just eaten as a snack.

One of my favourite snacks involves cutting courgette, carrots, celery, cucumber and bell pepper into batons and then serving them with a variety if dips. If you can make your own dips then great, but any shop bought dip including hummus works well with this.

Baked Cheesy Courgette

A delicious snack that is highly addictive. Although the recipe calls for Parmesan cheese, feel free to substitute this for whatever you have to hand or your favourite cheese.

Ingredients:
- 4 courgettes (quartered lengthwise)
- ½ cup Parmesan cheese (grated)
- 2 tablespoons fresh parsley leaves (chopped)
- 2 tablespoons olive oil
- ½ teaspoon dried basil
- ½ teaspoon dried oregano
- ½ teaspoon dried thyme
- ¼ teaspoon garlic powder
- Salt and freshly ground black pepper to taste

Method:
1. Preheat your oven to 350F / 175C
2. Coat a cooling rack with a non-stick spray, put it on a baking sheet and put to one side
3. In a small bowl, mix together everything except the courgette and olive oil, seasoning to taste with salt and pepper
4. Put the courgette onto the cooling rack on the baking sheet
5. Drizzle with olive oil, then sprinkle with the cheese mixture
6. Bake in your oven for around 15 minutes until tender
7. Put under your broiler or grill for a couple of minutes until they are crisp and brown
8. Serve immediately and garnish with chopped fresh parsley

Courgette Oven Fries

These are a great substitute for potato chips or French fries and are delicious and crispy.

Ingredients:
- 2½ cups courgette (sliced into ¼" slices)
- ¼ cup / 1oz Parmesan cheese (grated – substitute for an alternative if preferred)
- ¼ cup dry breadcrumbs
- 2 tablespoons fat-free milk
- ¼ teaspoon garlic powder
- ¼ teaspoon salt
- Few twists of freshly ground black pepper

Method:
1. Preheat your oven to 425F / 220C
2. Put everything except the milk and courgette into a medium bowl and combine well, using a whisk
3. Pour the milk into a shallow bowl
4. Dip the courgette into the milk and then dredge in the breadcrumb mixture until covered on both sides
5. Grease an ovenproof wire rack and place on a baking sheet
6. Place the coated courgette on the rack
7. Back for approximately 30 minutes until brown and crisp, finishing off under a grill or broiler if necessary

Pizza Bites

These are a delicious way to use up your courgettes. Be as adventurous as you like with the toppings, using any of your favourite pizza toppings. Although mozzarella is recommended, you can substitute for cheddar or an alternative cheese.

Ingredients:

- 3 courgettes (cut into ¼" slices)
- ½ cup mozzarella/cheddar (finely grated)
- 1/3 cup marinara sauce
- ¼ cup small pepperoni
- 1 tablespoon extra-virgin olive oil
- 1 tablespoon Italian seasoning
- Salt and black pepper to taste

Method:

1. Preheat your broiler/grill
2. Heat the olive oil in a large frying pan on a medium to high heat
3. Cook the courgette, in batches for a couple of minutes on each side until golden
4. Season to taste
5. Put the courgette slices onto a large, greased baking sheet
6. Spread some marinara sauce on each slice
7. Put on the pepperoni, or other pizza ingredients, then top with the grated cheese
8. Cook for a couple of minutes under your broiler
9. Serve immediately, sprinkled with Italian seasoning

Salt and Vinegar Chips

These are a great alternative to potato chips. Feel free to adjust the seasoning to your preferences; paprika makes for a great seasoning on these chips.

Ingredients:

- 4 medium courgettes (sliced very thinly – around an eighth of an inch thick)
- 2 tablespoons apple cider vinegar (can substitute red wine or white wine vinegar)
- 2 tablespoons olive oil
- ½ teaspoon fine salt
- ¼ teaspoon ground black pepper

Method:

1. Preheat your oven to 225F / 110C
2. Line two large baking sheets with silicone mats or parchment paper and spray oil onto them
3. Cut the courgette to size, use a food processor attachment or mandolin cutter to get a consistent thickness and for speed
4. Put everything except the courgette into a large bowl and whisk together
5. Add the courgette and gently stir to coat all of the courgette slices – do this in batches if it is easier
6. Remove the courgette from the bowl, starting with those at the bottom which will be better coated
7. Spread them out in a single layer on your baking trays, ensuring they do not overlap
8. Cook in the oven for 2 to 3 hours, until the courgette doesn't bend when lifted off the sheet
9. If some chips are done quicker than others, remove those that are done and cook the rest until done
10. Remove from the oven, cool on a wire rack and then store in an airtight container

Tasty Courgette Dip

This is a great dip, can be used at any event. The combination of courgette and herbs makes a very creamy, moreish dip that will be a big hit. Serve this with vegetable batons, bread, breadsticks or crackers.

Ingredients:
- 1 medium sized courgette (cubed)
- 1 garlic clove (chopped)
- 2 cups mayonnaise
- 2 tablespoons white (granulated) sugar
- 1 tablespoon soy sauce
- ¾ teaspoon dried oregano

Method:
1. Put the courgette into a saucepan, cover with water and bring to the boil
2. Cook for around 5 minutes until tender, then drain and pat dry
3. Put the courgette into your blender and process until smooth
4. Add the rest of the ingredients, except the mayonnaise and blend in
5. Put the mixture into a serving bowl and allow to cool a little
6. Stir in the mayonnaise and chill for an hour before serving

Cheesy Dip

Another great dip that is easy to make, tasty and works well with bread, crackers or vegetable batons.

Ingredients:
- 3 cups courgette (shredded)
- 2 cups Cheddar cheese (shredded)
- 1½ cups mayonnaise
- 1 cup pecans (chopped)
- 1/3 cup mozzarella cheese (shredded)
- ¼ cup red bell pepper (finely sliced)
- ¼ cup sour cream
- Salt and pepper to taste

Method:
1. In a medium bowl, mix together all of the ingredients
2. Add to your blender and process until smooth
3. Chill for an hour before using

Courgette & Corn Fritters

I really like these. These are a lovely, fluffy fritter that is a perfect accompaniment to any meal or great as a snack. Feel free to omit the cheese or substitute for a different one as you prefer. These are great served hot with a tangy ranch dressing.

Ingredients:

- 2 cups all-purpose (plain) flour
- 2 cups courgette (grated)
- 1½ cups fresh corn (ideally from the cob but canned will do)
- 1 cup milk
- 1 cup Cheddar cheese (finely shredded)
- ½ cup white (granulated) sugar
- ¼ cup butter (melted)
- 2 eggs (beaten)
- 1 tablespoon baking powder
- ½ teaspoon ground cumin
- ½ teaspoon salt

Method:

1. In a large bowl mix the flour with the cumin, sugar, salt, baking powder, and pepper
2. In a small bowl, mix the milk, butter, and eggs, whisking until thoroughly combined
3. Add the wet ingredients to the dry and whisk until thoroughly combined
4. Add the cheese, corn, and courgette, stirring well, ensuring they are evenly distributed and coated
5. Warm some oil in a large frying pan or skillet on a medium to high heat
6. Once the oil is hot, drop the batter in a tablespoon per fritter
7. Fry for a few minutes on either side until crisp and brown
8. Pat dry on paper towels and keep warm until serving

Courgette Pancakes
This is an interesting variation on the pancake, making a nice savoury dish. Instead of making your own batter mix, as this recipe describes, you can use a pre-made pancake mix for speed.

Ingredients:
- 4 eggs
- 2 cups courgette (grated)
- ¾ cup all-purpose (plain) flour
- ¼ cup butter (melted)
- 3 tablespoons extra-virgin olive oil
- 4 teaspoons baking powder
- ½ teaspoon white (granulated) sugar
- ½ teaspoon salt

Method:
1. Preheat your grill to between 425 to 450F (220-225C) or use a large frying pan to cook these
2. In a large bowl, beat the eggs
3. Add the courgette and stir well
4. Add everything except the baking powder and butter, stirring well, ensuring it is thoroughly combined
5. Add the baking powder and mix well to get a consistency like heavy whipping cream
6. Each pancake is table from about 2 tablespoons of batter
7. Cook for a couple of minutes on each side
8. Rub melted butter into both sides of the pancake and serve hot

MAIN DISH RECIPES

Although courgettes are usually used as a side dish, they can be used in a wide variety of main dishes. Most of the courgette you will buy are green, but if you can get yellow courgette, then this can add some nice colour to a dish.

Of course, courgettes can be used in a wide variety of other dishes as an additional ingredient from stir fries to pasta to ratatouille and more. These recipes all put the spotlight firmly on the courgette as the star of the show.

Pasta Primavera

This is a great dish, made with courgette noodles. Use a combination of yellow and green courgette for a wonderful colour.

Ingredients:
- 2 medium courgettes (spiralized into noodles)
- 2 medium carrots (peeled then cut into shavings using a vegetable peeler)
- 1 bell pepper (de-seeded and thinly sliced)
- ½ small red onion (peeled and thinly sliced)
- 1½ cups broccoli florets
- 1 cup cherry tomatoes (halved)
- ½ cup Parmesan cheese (grated) plus extra to garnish
- ½ cup frozen green peas (defrosted)
- 2 tablespoons lemon juice
- 2 tablespoons fresh parsley (chopped)
- 1 tablespoon extra-virgin olive oil
- 3 teaspoons minced garlic
- Pinch of red pepper flakes
- Salt and pepper to taste

Method:
1. Fill a medium saucepan with lightly salted water and bring to the boil
2. Add the broccoli and cook for about 2 minutes until tender but still crunchy
3. Drain, pat dry and put to one side
4. Heat the olive oil in a large frying pan or skillet on a medium heat
5. Add the onions, garlic and red pepper flakes, cooking, stirring regularly, for around 3 minutes until the onions become translucent
6. Add the bell pepper, tomatoes, and green peas, seasoning to taste
7. Cook for a further 3 minutes until the bell pepper becomes soft
8. Add the carrot, courgette, parsley and lemon juice
9. Cook, tossing regularly, for a further 3 minutes until the noodles are al denote
10. Add the cheese and broccoli, tossing to ensure the cheese is well distributed in the mixture
11. Serve in bowls, garnished with Parmesan cheese

Tuna and Chilli Linguine

Another great main course that is simple to make and very tasty. Remove the tuna and add other vegetables to turn this into a vegetarian-friendly meal.

Ingredients:
1. 12oz linguine pasta
2. 8oz mushrooms (any variety – thinly sliced)
3. 3 garlic cloves (finely chopped)
4. 2 medium courgettes (thinly sliced)
5. 2 fresh chillies (thinly sliced)
6. 3 tablespoons extra-virgin online oil
7. ½ teaspoon salt
8. Black pepper to taste
9. 6oz can tuna in olive oil (drained)

Method:
1. Cook the linguine as per the instructions, keeping ½ cup of the cooking water to one side
2. Heat the olive oil in a frying pan or skillet on a medium heat
3. Add the chillies and garlic, cooking for 2 minutes, stirring continuously
4. Add the mushrooms and courgette, seasoning to taste
5. Cook for a further 5 minutes, stirring often
6. Remove from the heat
7. In a large bowl, toss together the courgette, tuna, and linguini, adding any of the cooking water as required

Stuffed Courgette Boats

This is a great dish, stuffed with sausage meat. Use your favourite type of sausage for some variety. Alternatively, stuff with a vegetarian mixture. This is best served with pasta, garnished with fresh chopped parsley.

Ingredients:

- 4 small to medium courgettes
- 2 links of sweet Italian sausages (remove the casings)
- 1 small onion (chopped)
- 1¼ cups marinara sauce
- 1 cup mozzarella (shredded)
- 2 teaspoons extra-virgin olive oil
- ¼ teaspoon salt

Method:

1. Preheat your oven to 450F / 240C
2. Cut the courgettes in half lengthwise and scrape out the flesh, leaving around ¼" of the skin and flesh
3. Chop the removed flesh
4. Heat the oil in a large skillet on a medium to high heat
5. Add the onion, courgette flesh, salt, and sausage
6. Cook for approximately 8 minutes, breaking up any lumps with the back of a spoon
7. Spread the marinara sauce out in a baking dish
8. Arrange the courgette cases in this with the cut side up
9. Divide the sausage mixture evenly between the boats
10. Sprinkle with the shredded mozzarella
11. Cover with foil
12. Bake for 30 minutes before removing the cover and baking for a further 5 minutes to brown
13. Serve immediately

Vegetarian Pan Lasagne

This is a great meal to serve at a dinner party and is relatively simple to make. Serve garnished with torn fresh basil.

Ingredients:

- 28oz can crushed tomatoes
- 6oz lasagne noodles (no boil variety – broken into thirds)
- 3 garlic cloves (chopped)
- 1 onion (chopped)
- 1 red bell pepper (de-seeded and chopped)
- 1 courgette (sliced)
- 1 cup ricotta cheese
- 1 cup mozzarella cheese (shredded)

Method:

1. Heat the oil in a deep skillet or frying pan on a medium to high heat
2. Add the bell pepper, garlic, onion, and courgette
3. Cook for 6 minutes, stirring often
4. Reduce the heat and stir in the tomatoes
5. Add the noodles, making sure they are all submerged as much as possible
6. Cover and cook on a low heat for about 15 minutes, stirring occasionally, until the noodles are almost al dente
7. Spread the ricotta over the noodles and then sprinkle the mozzarella over this
8. Cover and cook for a further 10 minutes until the noodles are al dente and the cheese has melted
9. Season with black pepper and garnish with fresh basil when serving

Squash Gratin

Another interesting dish that is fun to make. Use whichever summer squash you can get hold of, or use additional courgettes if necessary. Feel free to substitute a different cheese for the Gruyere.

Ingredients:

- 2lb small courgette (top and tail, then half lengthwise)
- 2lb small yellow summer squash (top and tail, then half lengthwise)
- 2 garlic cloves(crushed)
- 1 cup Gruyere cheese (shredded)
- 1 cup whole milk
- 3 tablespoons all-purpose (plain) flour
- 2 tablespoons extra-virgin olive oil
- 2 tablespoons butter
- 1 teaspoon fresh thyme leaves
- ½ teaspoon salt and freshly ground black pepper

Method:

1. Heat a grill or broiler to a medium heat
2. In a large bowl, toss the squash and courgette in the oil before seasoning with the salt and pepper, stirring to ensure the vegetables are evenly coated
3. Grill the squash and courgette for 12 minutes until mostly tender, turning once
4. Remove from the grill and cool on a cutting board
5. Cook the garlic in the oil, stirring often, in a large pan on medium
6. Add the flour and cook for a further minute, stirring continuously
7. Whisk in the milk until the mixture is smooth
8. Stir in the thyme and season to taste
9. Reduce the heat and simmer for 1 to 2 minutes until thickened, then remove from the heat
10. Preheat your oven to 425F/220C and grease a baking dish
11. Thinly slice the squash and courgette, putting half of it in your baking dish
12. Press down gently and cover with half of the sauce
13. Layer the rest of the squash on top of this before covering with the remainder of the sauce
14. Top with the cheese
15. Bake for about 15 minutes, until the cheese browns then transfer to a broiler for a couple of minutes to finish browning
16. Stand for 5 minutes before serving

Courgette Lasagne

This alternative lasagne is not made with the usual noodles, but instead with cheese filled ravioli for a particularly decadent dish. In order to aid slicing, leave this to cool for between 5 and 10 minutes before slicing and serving.

Ingredients:

- 2 medium courgettes (sliced lengthwise)
- 1 small onion (diced)
- 1 pack of large, frozen cheese ravioli
- 1 jar of tomato and basil sauce
- 8oz lean ground beef
- 1 cup mozzarella cheese (shredded)
- ¼ cup Parmesan cheese (grated)
- 3 teaspoons extra-virgin olive oil

Method:

1. Preheat your oven to 375F/190C
2. Grease a 2-quart baking dish and line a cookie sheet with paper kitchen towels
3. Bring a large saucepan of water to the boil
4. Add the courgette and cook for around 5 minutes, then remove and drain on the prepared cookie sheet
5. Bring the water back to the boil and cook the ravioli until they rise to the top
6. In a separate saucepan, heat 2 teaspoons of oil on a medium heat
7. Cook the onion until lightly browned, around 8 to 10 minutes then put to one side in a bowl
8. Cook the beef with 1 teaspoon of oil until browned, around 3 to 4 minutes
9. Add the onion and jar of sauce, returning to the boil stirring often
10. Drain the ravioli and return it to the pan with the meat, stirring until thoroughly combined
11. In your baking dish, arrange half of the courgette on the bottom of the pan, pressing down lightly
12. Top with half of the ravioli, half the mozzarella, and half the Parmesan
13. Repeat the layering to use up the rest of the ingredients
14. Bake in your oven for 20 to 25 minutes until hot in the middle and golden brown on the top

Barbecue Lamb Salad

This is a nice main course or can be served on the side at a barbecue. You can swap the feta cheese for another if you prefer.

Ingredients:
- 9 lamb cutlets (French trimmed are best)
- 3 lemons (zest and juice 1 and cut the other two into 4 thick sliced)
- 4 scallions/spring onions (finely sliced)
- 1 red chilli (deseeded and finely chopped)
- 14oz / 400g can butter beans (rinsed and drained)
- 9oz / 250g baby courgettes
- 5oz / 140g feta cheese (crumbled)
- Small bunch of fresh mint leaves
- Extra-virgin olive oil

Method:
1. Put the lamb into a large bowl with 4 tablespoons olive oil and the lemon juice
2. Toss until well covered and then leave for around 20 minutes to marinate
3. Use 2 to 3 tablespoons of olive oil to brush the courgette and season to taste
4. Remove the lamb from the marinade and season to taste
5. Griddle or barbecue the lamb for 2 to 3 minutes per side
6. Griddle or barbecue the courgette for 2 to 3 minutes per side until tender and starting to char
7. Griddle or barbecue the lemon slices for 30 to 60 seconds per side until they start to caramelize and char
8. Arrange the lamb and courgette on a large plate
9. Scatter over the mint, butter beans, chilli, lemon zest, scallions, cheer and seasoning
10. Toss until well combined
11. Drizzle the olive oil over the mixture then add the cooked lemons to squeeze over the dish

Grilled Courgette Salad

A summer salad that is both warm and spicy. This is great as a tapas-style dish, though works as a lunch or a side for a main meal.

Ingredients:

- 2 courgettes (diagonally sliced)
- 1 red bell pepper (deseeded and cut in half)
- 14oz / 400g can butter beans (rinsed and drained)
- 100g small broad beans
- 100g fresh peas
- 100g cooking chorizo (skinned and diced)
- 1 tablespoon extra-virgin olive oil plus more to brush
- 1 teaspoon sherry vinegar
- ½ lemon (juiced)

Method:

1. Heat your grill or broiler to a high heat
2. Put the oil in a frying pan and heat on medium
3. Cook the chorizo for between 7 and 9 minutes until cooked through, and it has released its oil
4. Remove the chorizo from the pan, use a slotted spoon, and put to one side
5. Reduce the heat, add the vinegar and whisk before removing from the heat
6. Put the bell pepper cut side down on a baking sheet and grill for about 4 minutes until the skin blistered and chars
7. Transfer the pepper to a bowl and cover with plastic wrap
8. Once cooled, remove the skin and any seeds and tear it into strips
9. Cook the broad beans and peas in boiling water for 2 minutes then transfer to a bowl of iced water to cool quickly so they retain their colour
10. Drain and put to one side
11. Heat a griddle pan on a high heat
12. Brush the courgette with olive oil and cook on both sides for 1 to 2 minutes until tender, though not too soft
13. Put all of the ingredients into the pan with the dressing
14. Season to taste and toss well before serving

FUN WITH A SPIRALIZER

Spiralizers have become incredibly popular as a way to serve vegetables and make them more interesting. Typically, they come with some attachments which allow you to do anything from make vegetable noodles to making vegetable ribbons.

They are very versatile devices and a great way to turn 'boring' vegetables into something much more interesting. Here they are mainly used to turn courgette into noodles, but you can use them to make any salad more interesting. You will hear people calling courgette noodles 'zoodles, ' and these have become very trendy.

Spiralizers come in a manual or electric forms and at a variety of price points. Which you choose is entirely up to you and your budget. Both work and will produce great noodles!

Courgette noodles are becoming popular, particularly with Paleo diet followers, as they are lower in calories and carbohydrates than the usual grain based pasta. They are gently cooked, steamed or eaten raw, depending on your preference. Many people will cut their courgette noodles in half as they are often very long and can be difficult to eat due to their length.

Asian Courgette Noodle Salad

This is a great way to serve courgette noodles and makes for a great side dish, lunch or snack. Try making this with half courgette and half cucumber.

Ingredients:

- 3 medium courgettes (spiralized)
- 2 garlic cloves (crushed)
- ¼ cup fresh cilantro (packed and finely chopped)
- 3 tablespoons seasoned rice vinegar
- 1 tablespoon toasted sesame oil
- 2 teaspoons white (granulated) sugar
- 2 teaspoons crushed red pepper flakes
- ½ teaspoon salt

Method:

1. Mix all of the ingredients, except the courgette, together in a large bowl
2. Add the courgette, toss until thoroughly combined and then serve

Greek Style Noodle Salad

This is a Greek salad made with courgette noodles that makes a great lunch or side dish. Feel free to swap out the feta cheese for your favourite type of cheese, though grate it if you cannot crumble the substitute cheese.

Ingredients:
- 2 courgettes (spiralized)
- 10 cherry tomatoes (halved)
- 10 Kalamata olives (pitted and halved)
- ¼ cucumber (chopped)
- ¼ cup red onion (thinly sliced)
- 2oz feta cheese (crumbled)
- 2 tablespoons fresh lemon juice
- 2 tablespoons extra-virgin olive oil
- 1 teaspoon dried oregano
- Salt and pepper to taste

Method:
1. In a small bowl, whisk together the lemon juice, olive oil, and oregano together, seasoning to taste
2. Put the rest of the ingredients into a large bowl
3. Pour the dressing over the vegetables and toss, ensuring thoroughly coated
4. Marinate for around 15 minutes in your refrigerator before serving

Prawn Arrabbiata

This is a great dish that is Paleo diet friendly, served with courgette noodles. It is quick and easy to make, being great for a packed lunch.

Ingredients:

- 2 large courgettes (spiralized)
- 10½oz / 300g raw king prawns
- 3 garlic cloves (finely diced)
- 1 onion (finely chopped)
- ½ red bell pepper (finely diced)
- 1½ cups passata (substitute for chopped tomatoes for a chunkier sauce)
- ¼ cup Parmesan cheese (grated)
- 3 tablespoons extra-virgin olive oil
- 2/3 teaspoon chilli flakes
- 2/3 teaspoon salt
- Coconut oil
- Freshly chopped basil or parsley (for garnish)

Method:

1. Heat the coconut oil in a large pan on a high heat
2. Fry the prawns for 2 minutes, stirring occasionally, before removing from the pan and putting in a bowl
3. Reduce the heat to medium and pour the olive oil into the pan
4. Sauté the onions and peppers for about 3 minutes, until softened and lightly browned
5. Add the garlic, chilli and salt, stirring well
6. Pour in the passata, stir well and cook for a further 2 minutes, stirring occasionally
7. Add the courgette noodles and prawns, stirring for a couple of minutes until heated through (the courgette should soften a little and not become soggy)
8. Serve garnished with grated cheese and chopped herbs

Courgette Fettuccine

This is wonderful served with a creamy sauce based on butternut squash. Definitely worth a try. Feel free to use any other mushrooms if you cannot find shiitake mushrooms.

Ingredients:

- 4 medium sized courgettes (spiralized)
- 2 garlic cloves (minced)
- 1 yellow onion (chopped)
- 2 cups butternut squash (peeled and cubed)
- 1 cup vegetable/chicken broth
- 1 cup coconut milk (full or reduced fat)
- 6oz shiitake mushrooms (sliced)
- 1 tablespoon coconut oil
- 1 teaspoon dried rosemary (crushed)
- 1 teaspoon arrowroot powder
- ½ teaspoon sea salt

Method:

1. Put the onions, garlic, squash, broth, coconut milk, salt, and rosemary into a medium pot, stirring well
2. Bring to the boil, reduce the heat and cover, simmering for 15 to 25 minutes until the squash is tender
3. Pour into a blender and process until smooth
4. Put the sauce back into your pan and add the arrowroot powder, whisking until smooth
5. Simmer for a further 2 minutes until thickened
6. Remove from the heat and put to one side
7. Put the coconut oil into a medium sized frying pan on a medium heat
8. Cook the mushrooms for 2 to 3 minutes
9. Add the courgette and cook until tender, 3 to 5 minutes, stirring regularly
10. Drain the noodles, divide between plates, top with the sauce and serve

Turkey Bolognese

This is a traditional Italian Bolognese recipe, served on a bed of courgette noodles rather than spaghetti. Feel free to substitute any other meat or vegetarian option for the turkey, adjusting cooking time appropriately.

Ingredients:

- 3 medium courgettes (spiralized)
- 28oz can crushed tomatoes
- 1lb ground turkey
- ½ cup onion (finely diced)
- 3 tablespoons extra-virgin online oil (divided)
- 2 tablespoons tomato paste
- 1 tablespoon minced garlic
- 3 teaspoons white (granulated) sugar
- 1 teaspoon salt
- ½ teaspoon black pepper
- Grated Parmesan cheese (for serving)

Method:

1. Put two tablespoons of the oil into a large frying pan on a low to medium heat
2. Sauté the garlic and onions for 2 to 3 minutes until the onions become translucent, and the garlic turns a golden colour
3. Add the turkey and increase the heat to medium
4. Break the turkey up with your spatula and cook until browned
5. Add the tomato paste, crushed tomato, salt, pepper, and sugar
6. Reduce the heat and cook for around 10 minutes, stirring occasionally
7. Put 1 tablespoon of olive oil into another pan on a low to medium heat
8. Add the courgette noodles and cook, constantly tossing for about 2 minutes until they start to wilt
9. Divide the noodles between the plates, top with the Bolognese and garnish with grated cheese

Courgette Noodle Soup

This is an alternative chicken noodle soup made with courgette noodles rather than pasta noodles.

Ingredients:
- 1 large courgette (spiralized)
- 1 large carrot (peeled and spiralized)
- 2 celery sticks (half lengthwise and chop)
- 1-2 garlic cloves (minced)
- ½ white onion (chopped)
- 4 cups chicken broth
- 2 cups rotisserie chicken (or leftovers, shredded)
- 2 tablespoons extra-virgin olive oil
- 1 teaspoon fresh parsley (chopped)
- ½ teaspoon dried oregano
- 4 sprigs of thyme

Method:
1. Pour the olive oil into a large saucepan and heat on medium
2. Add the onion, celery, and garlic, seasoning to taste
3. Cook for between 3 and 5 minutes, stirring regularly until the vegetables start to soften
4. Add the parsley, oregano, thyme sprigs and chicken broth, stirring well
5. Turn the heat to high and boil, reducing to a low heat and simmer for a further 5 minutes
6. Add the carrot and chicken, cooking for a further 5 minutes
7. Add the courgette and cook for another minute or two until the noodles are slightly soft

Pesto Courgette Noodles
Another variation on the zoodle with a tasty pesto sauce.

Ingredients:
- 7oz jar sun-dried tomatoes in olive oil
- 2 garlic cloves (roughly chopped)
- 4 medium courgettes (spiralized)
- 1 cup fresh basil leaves (lightly packed)
- ¼ cup Parmesan cheese (shredded)
- 1 tablespoon extra-virgin online oil
- 1 tablespoon pine nuts (toasted)

Method:
1. Put the cheese, pine nuts, basil, garlic, tomatoes and their oil into your food processor
2. Process until puréed then season to taste with salt and pepper
3. Transfer to a large bowl and put to one side
4. Heat the olive oil in a large pan on a medium heat
5. Sauté the courgette with a pinch of salt for 2 to 3 minutes until just starting to soften
6. Add to the pesto, toss well and serve garnished with Parmesan cheese

Szechuan Zoodles

A fiery, spicy courgette noodle recipe that is worth making to impress dinner guests.

Ingredients:
- 6 baby bell peppers (sliced)
- 3 medium courgettes (spiralized)
- 1 chilli (sliced)
- ½lb spaghetti or linguine (substitute for extra courgette if preferred)
- 1 cup cherry tomatoes (halved)
- 1 cup fresh basil (chopped)
- ½ cup roasted peanuts (finely chopped)
- ½ cup fresh cilantro (chopped)
- ¼ cup peanut butter (creamy/smooth works best)
- ¼ cup tahini paste
- ¼ cup coconut milk
- 2 tablespoons soy sauce
- 2 tablespoons toasted sesame seeds
- 2 tablespoons lime juice
- 2 tablespoons honey / brown sugar
- 1 tablespoon hot chilli oil
- 2 teaspoons toasted sesame oil

Method:
1. Cook the pasta until al dente in boiling salted water, drain and keep warm
2. In a large bowl whisk together the peanut butter and tahini
3. Add the chilli oil, lime juice, soy sauce, honey, coconut milk and sesame oil, whisking well
4. Add in the zoodles, sesame seeds, basil, peanuts, bell peppers, tomatoes and cilantro, stirring well
5. Stir in the pasta and toss until thoroughly combined
6. Serve topped with basil, peanuts and/or hot pepper slices according to preference

Pad Thai Zoodles

This is best made with the courgette noodles being slightly crunchy, so be careful not to overcook them. Use whatever protein you want such as shrimp, chicken, beef, tofu or anything else.

Pad Thai Ingredients:
- 3 garlic cloves (minced or crushed)
- 3 green onions (sliced)
- 2 medium courgettes (spiralized)
- 1 large egg
- ½ red bell pepper (thinly sliced)
- ½lb / 225g protein
- 2 cups / 480ml bean sprouts
- 1/3 cup / 80ml roasted peanuts
- ¼ cup cilantro (chopped)
- Lime wedges for serving

Sauce Ingredients:
- 3 tablespoons ketchup
- 2 tablespoons fish sauce
- 2 tablespoons rice vinegar
- 1 teaspoon chilli garlic sauce
- 1 teaspoon brown sugar (packed)
- ½ teaspoon cayenne pepper

Method:
1. In a small bowl, mix together all of the sauce ingredients and put to one side
2. Heat a tablespoon of the oil in a large pan
3. Cook the courgette noodles for 2 or 3 minutes until tender, avoiding overcooking
4. Leave to rest for 3 to 4 minutes then remove from the pan, then drain off excess water
5. Wipe the pan, removing excess water before reheating on a medium to high heat
6. Add the rest of the olive oil and sauté the garlic for 30-60 seconds until soft and translucent
7. Add the protein and cook as required until cooked through
8. Add the green onions and bell peppers, cooking for 2-3 minutes until tender
9. Stir in the egg and cook for a further 1 to 2 minutes until the egg is

cooked
10. Add the sauce and zoodles, cooking for another minute until heated throughout
11. Stir in the bean sprouts
12. Serve immediately garnished with lime wedges, roasted peanuts, and cilantro

Roasted Corn Salad

The combination of tastes and textures in this salad works wonderfully, making this a perfect summer salad.

Ingredients:

- 2 large courgettes (spiralized)
- 2 corn on the cob
- ½ large red onion (diced)
- Salt and pepper to season

Vinaigrette Ingredients:

- 1 tablespoon extra-virgin online oil
- ½ tablespoon apple cider vinegar
- 1 teaspoon honey
- 1 teaspoon garlic powder
- ¾ teaspoon salt
- ½ teaspoon chilli powder
- ½ teaspoon pepper
- Zest and juice of 1 lime

Method:

1. Spray corn cobs with cooking oil and season to taste with salt and pepper
2. Grill for a few minutes, turning regularly, until slightly charred
3. Put all the vinaigrette ingredients into a bowl and mix until thoroughly combined
4. Remove the kernels from the corn when cooled
5. Add the zoodles, corn, and onion to a large bowl
6. Pour over the vinaigrette and toss until thoroughly covered

ENDNOTE

Courgettes are a wonderfully versatile vegetable that can be surprisingly expensive to buy in the shops, yet incredibly easy to grow at home. It is a prolific fruiter and we all plant half a dozen or so plants, thinking that may just be enough before being utterly overwhelmed by the sheer volume of fruits produced by the plant.

Although the yellow courgettes do not grow too big, some of the green varieties will appear to turn into monsters overnight. Courgettes are best picked before they grow too big as the skin becomes tougher and the seeds grow larger, making it less pleasant to eat. However, don't despair if your courgette grows too big as you can peel them and scoop out the middle where the seeds are. Don't worry, that overgrown courgette can still be eaten, meaning even more ideas are needed!

I find growing a variety of courgettes, both the green, yellow and round varieties makes for more interesting meals. Although the yellow courgettes are not yellow all the way through, the combination of yellow and green skins can make for a colourful dish. The round courgettes are great if you cut the top off them, scoop out the insides and then stuff it with your favourite mixture of rice, vegetables, spices, and meat.

There are lots of recipes in this book, and there are plenty more out there. These are my favourite recipes and the ones that I feel make the most interesting use of your courgettes. As you will find plenty of them on your plants, you can try all of the different recipes, which means you aren't going to get bored with them! I can particularly recommend the chocolate cake as that is out of this world, and no one will believe it has courgette in it. Another favourite of mine is the courgette pizza slices or boats. These have been a huge hit with anyone I have served them to, even people who don't normally like courgette!

Enjoy experimenting with these recipes and cooking your courgettes. Feel free to Tweet or Instagram me pictures of your culinary exploits at #allotmentowner. Have great fun cooking the wide variety of dishes in this book, there really is something for everyone and every occasion.

ABOUT JASON

Jason has been a keen gardener for over twenty years, having taken on numerous weed infested patches and turned them into productive vegetable gardens.

One of his first gardening experiences was digging over a 400 square foot garden in its entirety and turning it into a vegetable garden, much to the delight of his neighbors who all got free vegetables! It was through this experience that he discovered his love of gardening and started to learn more and more about the subject.

His first encounter with a greenhouse resulted in a tomato infested greenhouse but he soon learnt how to make the most of a greenhouse and now grows a wide variety of plants from grapes to squashes to tomatoes and more. Of course, his wife is delighted with his greenhouse as it means the windowsills in the house are no longer filled with seed trays every spring.

He is passionate about helping people learn to grow their own fresh produce and enjoy the many benefits that come with it, from the exercise of gardening to the nutrition of freshly picked produce. He often says that when you've tasted a freshly picked tomato you'll never want to buy another one from a store again!

Jason is also very active in the personal development community, having written books on self-help, including subjects such as motivation and confidence. He has also recorded over 80 hypnosis programs, being a fully qualified clinical hypnotist which he sells from his website www.MusicForChange.com.

He hopes that this book has been a pleasure for you to read and that you have learned a lot about the subject and welcomes your feedback either directly or through an Amazon review. This feedback is used to improve his books and provide better quality information for his readers.

Jason also loves to grow giant and unusual vegetables and is still planning on breaking the 400lb barrier with a giant pumpkin. He hopes that with his new allotment plot he'll be able to grow even more exciting vegetables to share with his readers.

OTHER BOOKS BY JASON

Please check out my other gardening books on Amazon, available in Kindle and paperback.

Berry Gardening – The Complete Guide to Berry Gardening from Gooseberries to Boysenberries and More
Who doesn't love fresh berries? Find out how you can grow many of the popular berries at home such as marionberries and blackberries and some of the more unusual like honeyberries and goji berries. A step by step guide to growing your own berries including pruning, propagating and more. Discover how you can grow a wide variety of berries at home in your garden or on your balcony.

Canning and Preserving at Home – A Complete Guide to Canning, Preserving and Storing Your Produce
A complete guide to storing your home-grown fruits and vegetables. Learn everything from how to freeze your produce to canning, making jams, jellies, and chutneys to dehydrating and more. Everything you need to know about storing your fresh produce, including some unusual methods of storage, some of which will encourage children to eat fresh fruit!

Companion Planting Secrets – Organic Gardening to Deter Pests and Increase Yield
Learn the secrets of natural and organic pest control with companion planting. This is a great way to increase your yield, produce better quality plants and work in harmony with nature. By attracting beneficial insects to your garden, you can naturally keep down harmful pests and reduce the damage they cause. You probably grow many of these companion plants already, but by repositioning them, you can reap the many benefits of this natural method of gardening.

Container Gardening - Growing Vegetables, Herbs & Flowers in Containers

A step by step guide showing you how to create your very own container garden. Whether you have no garden, little space or you want to grow specific plants, this book guides you through everything you need to know about planting a container garden from the different types of pots, to which plants thrive in containers to handy tips helping you avoid the common mistakes people make with containers.

Environmentally Friendly Gardening – Your Guide to a Sustainable, Eco-Friendly Garden

With a looming environmental crisis, we are all looking to do our bit to save the environment. This book talks you through how to garden in harmony with nature and reduce your environmental impact. Learn how to eliminate the need for chemicals with clever techniques and eco-friendly alternatives. Discover today how you can become a more environmentally friendly gardener and still have a beautiful garden.

Greenhouse Gardening - A Beginners Guide to Growing Fruit and Vegetables All Year Round

A complete, step by step guide to owning your own greenhouse. Learn everything you need to know from sourcing greenhouses to building foundations to ensuring it survives high winds. This handy guide will teach you everything you need to know to grow a wide range of plants in your greenhouse, including tomatoes, chilies, squashes, zucchini and much more. Find out how you can benefit from a greenhouse today, they are more fun and less work than you might think!

Growing Brassicas – Growing Cruciferous Vegetables from Broccoli to Mooli to Wasabi and More

Brassicas are renowned for their health benefits and are packed full of vitamins. They are easy to grow at home but beset by problems. Find out how you can grow these amazing vegetables at home, including the incredibly beneficial plants broccoli and maca. Includes step by step growing guides plus delicious recipes for every recipe!

Growing Chilies – A Beginners Guide to Growing, Using & Surviving Chilies
Ever wanted to grow super-hot chilies? Or maybe you just want to grow your own chilies to add some flavor to your food? This book is your complete, step-by-step guide to growing chilies at home. With topics from selecting varieties to how to germinate seeds, you will learn everything you need to know to grow chilies successfully, even the notoriously difficult to grow varieties such as Carolina Reaper. With recipes for sauces, meals and making your own chili powder, you'll find everything you need to know to grow your own chili plants

Growing Fruit: The Complete Guide to Growing Fruit at Home
This is a complete guide to growing fruit from apricots to walnuts and everything in between. You will learn how to choose fruit plants, how to grow and care for them, how to store and preserve the fruit and much more. With recipes, advice, and tips this is the perfect book for anyone who wants to learn more about growing fruit at home, whether beginner or experienced gardener.

Growing Garlic – A Complete Guide to Growing, Harvesting & Using Garlic
Everything you need to know to grow this popular plant. Whether you are growing normal garlic or elephant garlic for cooking or health, you will find this book contains all the information you need. Traditionally a difficult crop to grow with a long growing season, you'll learn the exact conditions garlic needs, how to avoid the common problems people encounter and how to store your garlic for use all year round. A complete, step-by-step guide showing you precisely how to grow garlic at home.

Growing Herbs – A Beginners Guide to Growing, Using, Harvesting and Storing Herbs
A comprehensive guide to growing herbs at home, detailing 49 different herbs. Learn everything you need to know to grow these herbs from their preferred soil conditions to how to harvest and propagate them and more. Including recipes for health and beauty plus delicious dishes to make in your kitchen. This step-by-step guide is designed to teach you all about growing herbs at home, from a few herbs in containers to a fully-fledged herb garden. An indispensable guide to growing and using herbs.

Growing Giant Pumpkins – How to Grow Massive Pumpkins at Home

A complete step by step guide detailing everything you need to know to produce pumpkins weighing hundreds of pounds, if not edging into the thousands! Anyone can grow giant pumpkins at home, and this book gives you the insider secrets of the giant pumpkin growers showing you how to avoid the mistakes people commonly make when trying to grow a giant pumpkin. This is a complete guide detailing everything from preparing the soil to getting the right seeds to germinating the seeds and caring for your pumpkins.

Growing Lavender: Growing, Using, Cooking and Healing with Lavender

A complete guide to growing and using this beautiful plant. Find out about the hundreds of different varieties of lavender and how you can grow this bee friendly plant at home. With hundreds of uses in crafts, cooking and healing, this plant has a long history of association with humans. Discover today how you can grow lavender at home and enjoy this amazing herb.

Growing Tomatoes: Your Guide to Growing Delicious Tomatoes at Home

This is the definitive guide to growing delicious and fresh tomatoes at home. Teaching you everything from selecting seeds to planting and caring for your tomatoes as well as diagnosing problems this is the ideal book for anyone who wants to grow tomatoes at home. A comprehensive must have guide.

How to Compost – Turn Your Waste into Brown Gold

This is a complete step by step guide to making your own compost at home. Vital to any gardener, this book will explain everything from setting up your compost heap to how to ensure you get fresh compost in just a few weeks. A must have handbook for any gardener who wants their plants to benefit from home-made compost.

How to Grow Potatoes - The Guide to Choosing, Planting and Growing in Containers Or the Ground

Learn everything you need to know about growing potatoes at home. Discover the wide variety of potatoes you can grow, many delicious varieties you will never see in the shops. Find out the best way to grow potatoes at home, how to protect your plants from the many pests and diseases and how to store your harvest so you can enjoy fresh potatoes over winter. A complete step by step guide telling you everything you need to know to grow potatoes at home successfully.

Hydroponics: A Beginners Guide to Growing Food without Soil
Hydroponics is growing plants without soil, which is a fantastic idea for indoor gardens. It is surprisingly easy to set up, once you know what you are doing and is significantly more productive and quicker than growing in soil. This book will tell you everything you need to know to get started growing flowers, vegetables, and fruit hydroponically at home.

Indoor Gardening for Beginners: The Complete Guide to Growing Herbs, Flowers, Vegetables and Fruits in Your House
Discover how you can grow a wide variety of plants in your home. Whether you want to grow herbs for cooking, vegetables or a decorative plant display, this book tells you everything you need to know. Learn which plants to keep in your home to purify the air and remove harmful chemicals and how to successfully grow plants from cacti to flowers to carnivorous plants.

Keeping Chickens for Beginners – Keeping Backyard Chickens from Coops to Feeding to Care and More
Chickens are becoming very popular to keep at home, but it isn't something you should leap into without the right information. This book guides you through everything you need to know to keep chickens from decided what breed to what coop to how to feed them, look after them and keep your chickens healthy and producing eggs. This is your complete guide to owning chickens, with absolutely everything you need to know to get started and successfully keep chickens at home.

Raised Bed Gardening – A Guide to Growing Vegetables In Raised Beds
Learn why raised beds are such an efficient and effortless way to garden as you discover the benefits of no-dig gardening, denser planting and less bending, ideal for anyone who hates weeding or suffers from back pain. You will learn everything you need to know to build your own raised beds, plant them and ensure they are highly productive.

Save Our Bees – Your Guide to Creating a Bee Friendly Environment
Discover the plight of our bees and why they desperately need all of our help. Find out all about the different bees, how they are harmless, yet a vital part of our food chain. This book teaches you all about bees and how you can create a bee friendly environment in your neighborhood. You will learn the plants bees love, where they need to live and what plants are dangerous for bees, plus lots, lots more.

Vertical Gardening: Maximum Productivity, Minimum Space
This is an exciting form of gardening allows you to grow large amounts of fruit and vegetables in small areas, maximizing your use of space. Whether you have a large garden, an allotment or just a small balcony, you will be able to grow more delicious fresh produce. Find out how I grew over 70 strawberry plants in just three feet of ground space and more in this detailed guide.

Worm Farming: Creating Compost at Home with Vermiculture
Learn about this amazing way of producing high-quality compost at home by recycling your kitchen waste. Worms break it down and produce a sought after, highly nutritious compost that your plants will thrive in. No matter how big your garden you will be able to create your own worm farm and compost using the techniques in this step-by-step guide. Learn how to start worm farming and producing your own high-quality compost at home.

WANT MORE INSPIRING GARDENING IDEAS?

This book is part of the Inspiring Gardening Ideas series. Bringing you the best books anywhere on how to get the most from your garden or allotment. Please remember to leave a review on Amazon once you have finished this book as it helps me continually improve my books.

You can find out about more wonderful books just like this one at: www.GardeningWithJason.com

Follow me at www.YouTube.com/OwningAnAllotment for my video diary and tips. Join me on Facebook for regular updates and discussions at www.Facebook.com/OwningAnAllotment.

Find me on Instagram and Twitter as @allotmentowner where I post regular updates, offers and gardening news. Follow me today and let's catch up in person!

FREE BOOK!

ENVIRONMENTALLY
FRIENDLY
GARDENING

YOUR GUIDE TO A SUSTAINABLE,
ECO-FRIENDLY GARDEN

JASON JOHNS

Visit http://gardeningwithjason.com/your-free-book/ now for your free copy of my book "Environmentally Friendly Gardening" sent to your inbox. Discover today how you can become a more eco-friendly gardener and help us all make the world a better place.

This book is full of tips and advice, helping you to reduce your need for chemicals and work in harmony with nature to improve the environment. With the looming crisis, there is something we can all do in our gardens, no matter how big or small they are and they can still look fantastic!

Thank you for reading!